HOW TO RAISE A
HAPPY CAT

HOW TO RAISE A
HAPPY
CAT

SO THEY LOVE YOU MORE
THAN ANYONE ELSE

SOPHIE COLLINS

IVY PRESS

Brimming with creative inspiration, how-to projects, and useful information to enrich your everyday life, quarto.com is a favourite destination for those pursuing their interests and passions.

First published in 2023 by Ivy Press
an imprint of The Quarto Group.
One Triptych Place, London, SE1 9SH
United Kingdom
T (0)20 7700 6700
www.QuartoKnows.com

A catalogue record for this book is available from the British Library.

ISBN 978-0-7112-8179-0
EBOOK ISBN 978-0-7112-8181-3

10 9 8 7 6 5 4 3 2 1

Designer Ginny Zeal
Illustrator Kelsey Oseid

Printed in China

CONTENTS

INTRODUCTION

Despite being saddled with a number of clichés – 'mysterious' and 'inscrutable' are two of the most common – cats have been living alongside humans for a very long time (around 12,000 years at the current estimate), and it's likely that your own cat's behaviour is not entirely inscrutable, or at least not to you. If you've shared your space for a while, you probably know whether or not they're at ease with their surroundings, you'll able to spot the signs of what you'd interpret as specific moods, and you'll be familiar with their preferences when it comes to food and napping spots.

However, cats aren't close to being truly domesticated in the sense that pet dogs are, and for many that quality is what makes them the most interesting of 'companion' animals. Their unique status with humans comes from the fact that cats call the shots: while they're far from untrainable, they rarely seem to do things purely to please and, while plenty of dogs give a convincing impression of doting dependency on their people, cats don't generally respond to human attention in such an undignified way – although they certainly appreciate the access to food and warmth that people provide and, approached in the right way, will often enjoy interaction. Because many people make the assumption that cats are happily self-sufficient, they don't always give a lot of thought to the ways in which they approach their cats for play or affection, and they may not be fluent enough in feline body language to read positive or negative signs – which is a pity, because the human/cat relationship can blossom with more mutual understanding.

The limits of research

As yet, cats haven't been the focus of as much detailed research as dogs, either. We know more about dogs because they've been the subject of many, many studies, particularly over the last few decades when they've become the stars of behavioural research. Cats, generally more independent and less immediately cooperative with human efforts, have never commanded the same attention. Much of what we don't know about cats remains a mystery only because no one has yet taken the trouble to find out. Research is catching up, slowly but surely, and more scientific proof around what were previously assumptions about cat behaviour is emerging all the time.

An observant cat, tucked into the familiar 'loaf' shape (paws and tail tucked in and under), has perfected the art of staying warm as they watch.

Happy cat, happy caregiver

Cats seem to be good at being happy, or at least content, but as an owner you can certainly play your part, and *How to Raise a Happy Cat* sets out to help. The book is arranged in six sections:

• The first chapter, **A closer look**, examines what we know about how cats work, with their heritage, senses and body language put into context to allow you – as far as possible – to imagine yourself in your cat's paws.

• Chapters on specific aspects of a cat's experience follow, **Playing & enrichment**, **Staying fit & well**, **Eating** and **Rest & relaxation**, with lots of ideas for ways to interact with your cat and introduce enrichment to every aspect of their everyday life.

• **Life stages**, the final chapter, looks at some particular aspects of the different stages of a cat's life, from kitten to veteran, ensuring that you're looking out for your pet's lifelong happiness.

A CLOSER LOOK

How does your cat work? Very broadly, cats have the same systems and the same senses as us – that is to say, they're mammals and they see, hear, smell, taste and feel – but we know that they experience the world around them in quite a different way from humans, although research into domestic cats is still at a relatively early stage. This chapter takes a journey around your cat, from whisker ends to tail tip, looking in detail at what we already know about them – and speculating on what there may still be to find out.

CAT WORLD

Is it possible for a human to get a good idea of what a cat's *umwelt* might be? *Umwelt* describes the individual worlds that different species occupy – their environment, outlook and surroundings – both physically and in the sense of your world view.

Inevitably, our own *umwelt* is human and, as with all our pets, we tend to project our anthropomorphic thoughts and feelings onto our cats. However, with a little more knowledge of how cats and their senses work, it becomes easier for us to get at least a glimpse into their world.

Practical design

We can start by looking at where the domestic cat began. If you go back far enough – all the way to the Eocene era – dogs and cats shared a common ancestor (which looked rather more like a modern weasel), but the family branch split off 43 million years ago, after which, down thousands and thousands of generations, wild cats gradually evolved. The ancestors of *Felis catus*, today's pet, were small, solitary predators, and their specialized sight, scent and hearing developed primarily to help them hunt.

Some level of domestication arrived at the same time as humans began to grow crops in what is now known as the Middle East, at which point the USP of cats – their taste for rats and mice and their ability to catch them – became evident to humans. Farmers store grain, and anything that reduces the rodent population around granaries is welcome. No cat owner will be surprised that cats gained this sort of semi-domesticated status on their own terms, under a 'will hunt for food' agreement; not for them the multi-tasking – tracking and guarding, as well as hunting – that the dog had already brought to the household. Physically, it seems that not very much about them has changed since; in evolutionary terms, it's only a moment since they became welcome visitors to ancient granaries.

Sense by sense

To see the world through your cat's eyes, therefore, you must imagine yourself into the paws of an agile, acrobatic hunter with a strong reliance on specialized hearing, scenting ability and sight, all of which are wired differently from their human equivalents. Most of the natural behaviour we see when we play with our cats – or watch them playing with each other, or on their own – is associated with finely tuned hunting skills, whether or not your pet cat is still putting them to practical use. The following pages look at these senses, at how they would have been used in the wild, and at how we see their echoes in the pets of today.

OPPOSITE: Cats and people have a different balance of sensory intake, so it's difficult for us to imagine ourselves into a cat's direct experience of the world.

HOW THE WORLD SMELLS

If you were to rank your senses in order of importance, smell would probably lag behind. Your cat, on the other hand, would be likely to lead with it. In fact, cats may not be far behind dogs in scenting ability; science is only just catching up with them.

A rainbow of scents

A large number of mammals have much better developed – and practised – scenting abilities than humans; tested against coyotes, wolves and bears, to name only a few, we would perform very poorly indeed. When it comes to comparing our sense of smell with that of our cats, therefore, humans rather than cats are the exception to the mammalian rule. We know that cats smell much, much more acutely than we do; what we don't know yet is exactly how much more acutely. But since they have more than double the number of olfactory receptor cells, it's certain that their scent landscape is much more delicate and nuanced than ours (it's been predicated that a cat 'sees' subtleties in scent in the same way that humans see very fine gradations in colour).

How it's done

The cat breathes in scent molecules, where they are moistened by the warm air inside the nose and carried onto the mucous surface covering the olfactory nerves, site of the receptor cells, where they are sorted and their messages carried to the brain for interpretation – a process that happens in nanoseconds.

What's more, cats have an additional, separate scenting system, held in the vomeronasal, or Jacobson's, organ, above the roof of the mouth. Many animals have this separate system, but it seems to be used for different purposes according to species. In the case of cats, it appears to be dedicated to managing species-specific smells and probably developed because in the original state of things most cats lived fairly solitary lives, usually coming together only for to breed. The vomeronasal organ brings its owner news of the boundary markings of other cats – whether strangers or relations – the scents of possible mates, and so on. You have probably seen your cat using this secondary system, although you may not have known what they were doing: they will curl their lip slightly, revealing their teeth, and open their mouth a little – this last leads it to be called the gape response (it's also called the Flehmen response). A cat may stay in this position for a few seconds, presumably to analyse the details of the smell they're trying to pin down.

Leaving scent

To 'read' a scent, it has to have been left in the first place. Cats scent their surroundings generously, sometimes in ways we don't want (no household welcomes a marking tomcat), but much more often in ways that our own sense of smell is too blunt to detect. Every time a cat rubs against something in their immediate surroundings, they are leaving their own marking of scent from glands on their forehead, cheeks and chin. There's every reason to believe that this is not only a signal to others, but also a comforting signifier to themselves that they're at home.

OPPOSITE: We know that cats have an extremely acute sense of smell. To measure just how acute is going to take more dedicated research.

HOW THE WORLD LOOKS

A cat's eyes are very different to our own. For a start, they are enormous in proportion to the size of their head – human eyes enlarged to the same ratio would resemble an extreme manga drawing. And this is just one example of the many differences.

Eyes of a hunter

Historically, cats' naturally crepuscular lifestyle – they're much more active in the hours around dawn and dusk than in the middle of the day – meant that to be able to hunt, they needed to be able to sense small movements in very low light levels. During daylight hours they'd be more likely to be sleeping than hunting, so they had less need to see well, or to distinguish between fine colour gradations in brighter light. Developing to match these needs, the retinas of cats' eyes have a lot of rod cells (up to eight times as many as humans), which help vision at lower light levels, but far fewer cone cells (around a tenth of the number in human eyes), which are used to see differences in colour and movement in daylight.

In response to dim light, cats also have the ability to enlarge their pupils hugely: the narrow slit that you see in daylight can stretch to a near-circle in the dark to let in any and all the light available. Light that misses the retina and its receptor cells reflects off the *tapetum lucidum*, an extra layer at the back of the eye, and goes back through the retina, giving it a second chance to hit the receptors and maximize the amount of light received. Any 'wasted' light that bounces off the *tapetum lucidum* but doesn't hit receptor cells is reflected back out of the eyes and causes that eerie glow-in-the-dark effect when you meet a cat out at night

OPPOSITE: Your ability to see colour and detail falls fast in a low light, but cats' eyes have evolved to help them spot the slightest movement, even as daylight fades.

Finally, cats also have a slightly wider field of vision, at 200 degrees, against 180 degrees in humans, meaning that they're better than us at spotting movement out of the corner of their eye.

Daytime vision

This outstanding nocturnal vision has some payback when it comes to what cats can see in daylight. Cats' close-up vision is poor, with a notable weak spot up to around 30cm (12in) in front of them; this seems to be because their super-sized eyes have equally large lenses that aren't adaptable. A human eye has a lens that can be squeezed and pulled by surrounding muscles to bring things into focus; the lens in a cat's eye has to be moved in its entirety to focus on something. You may have seen your cat suddenly seem to notice something nearby, and it's likely that what you're watching is them focusing on that particular object in order to see it clearly.

HOW THE WORLD SOUNDS

A fine muscular system means that your cat's ears can be swivelled through 180 degrees towards interesting noises, allowing them to take in as much as possible. And although kittens are born with their ear canals closed, within weeks their hearing surpasses ours.

The widest range

The structure of a cat's ear is similar to that of other mammals. It divides into:

- the exterior ear, which is the upright flap of the pinna, and the ear canal behind it;
- the middle ear, consisting of the eardrum and the ossicles, a system of tiny bones that communicate vibrations to the inner ear;
- the inner ear itself, which manages the signals sent to the brain through the auditory nerve, and which also contains the vestibular system which controls a cat's balance and their sense of their body in the space around it.

The squeaks of a bat's echolocation are inaudibly high for human ears, but still fall within the upper limit of a cat's hearing.

A cat's ear flap, or pinna, starts editing a sound as soon as it's received: it is lined with very fine ridges that begin to process noises before they reach the ear canal, and can communicate (in a way which isn't yet fully understood) not only the nature of the sound, but also the level it is coming from. Cats have been shown to know how high the source of a sound is, as well as its specific direction – obviously an invaluable extra when it comes to pinpointing and catching your next meal.

What really sets a cat's hearing apart, though, is its range – it can hear sounds an octave and a half higher than a human can, but it can also hear very low sounds and distinguish between them. This is unusual because hearing that's adapted to ultrasound doesn't generally also cover the lower end of the scale. What enables this is the structure of the resonating chamber behind the cat's eardrum: in most mammals this forms a single space, but in cats it's divided into two parts, allowing its owner to process both high and low frequencies separately. Cats can hear noises across more than ten octaves, which is one more even than dogs, themselves renowned for their sharp ears.

What's it all for?

Just like their other senses, cats' hearing evolved for nocturnal hunting. They needed to be able to hear the very high communicating sounds of small rodents and bats, and to get close enough for a successful kill, because, unlike dogs, cats don't chase or track their prey but rely on a swift pounce from nearby. The result is a very rich soundscape for cats – add this refined hearing to their exceptional sense of smell, and you can imagine that when you see a cat 'just sitting', they're actually enjoying a sensory feast that is inaudible to our blunt human ears.

HOW THE WORLD FEELS

Cats are sensitive to even small changes in the space around them. They twitch and shiver at tiny alterations in temperature and texture, and they're hyper-aware of how narrow a gap they can squeeze through. Much of this is down to their whiskers.

As your cat 'captures' their toy, they will be using the sensitive whiskers at the back of their forelegs to position it minutely – important in a real hunt with living prey.

A sensory forcefield

Whiskers, or vibrissae, to give them their scientific name, are stiffened hairs that grow in spaced patterns along a cat's brow line, on their muzzle, under their chin and, much less noticeably, on the backs of their forelegs. They're fine monitors of movement – they can even detect changes in temperature They grow from nerve-rich follicles and although they're stiffer than regular coat hairs, they're also extremely flexible, so can be used to judge the space around a cat. For example, cats use their whiskers as guides to whether they can fit through a small space or not. Essentially they create an invisible field around the head and forebody of a cat, which makes the cat aware of anything around them just before it makes contact. Cats also have the same number of whiskers on both sides of the body, meaning that they're kept in sensory balance; although whiskers have a life span and are occasionally shed, replacements will quickly grow in the same spot.

How whiskers work

Whiskers are around three times thicker than regular cat hairs, with deeper roots. Each whisker can be moved independently by muscles at its root, but their length tends to depend on the size of the cat – the bigger the cat, the longer its whiskers are likely to be.

Whiskers as hunting aids

The need for whiskers around the face is fairly self-evident, but why do cats have the sensitive hairs on their legs? Of course they're useful to pick up clues about an environment as the cat walks, leaps or climbs through it, but these are another legacy of their lives as hunters – after a cat has pounced and landed successfully on a mouse, it's important that the prey can't escape, and, while the claws will be used to grip it, it's the sensitive whiskers at the back of the forelegs that judge how much resistance is left. You'll see this watching a cat play with a small toy – there are brief, assessing pauses, when the cat seems to be feeling, rather than clawing at its toy. These may be indications that it's 'testing' the toy with its vibrissae for any fightback.

To some extent, whiskers can be used as mood indicators, too; you may have noticed that whiskers held in the 'easy' position, at a near right-angle from your cat's face, indicates a relaxed pet, while a ruffled or upset cat will have their whiskers drawn back more tightly against their cheeks.

PAY ATTENTION
THE KIND CATS LIKE

You're probably familiar with your cat's body language: you know when they want to interact with you, and whether that means they want to play, or to be stroked or cuddled. Yet most of us don't pay enough attention to the day-to-day activities of our cats.

Low maintenance or unnoticed?

One of the reasons why there are more pet cats than dogs in the world is that cats don't demand the same levels of attention. Many cats are fed and 'noticed' briefly around mealtimes but don't get much attention for the rest of the day – they have toys and potential activities to occupy them (more

A very relaxed cat may welcome a chest massage, although the person who moves in for a belly scratch is either very brave or very familiar with that particular cat.

sleeping, looking out of the window, squeezing themselves into unimaginably tiny spaces), the thinking goes, and they don't need more than that. This isn't conscious unkindness, and there a few actively anti-social cats who probably prefer things that way, but most cats like attention and like to have interest in their lives and, given the chance, will enjoy a closer relationship with you.

The basics

The following chapters include plenty of ideas for giving your cat new experiences and enjoyments. As interest in the behaviour and cognitive powers of cats has grown, so has the concern that many pet cats lead quite boring lives, in environments that are reliable and safe but not really stimulating enough for an intelligent animal with highly developed senses. That's why the word 'enrichment' has become fashionable, and why owners are being encouraged to pay more day-to-day attention to their cats.

Keeping things gentle

To the human eye, cats don't have 'expressions' in the way dogs do – hence the often-used inscrutability label. There's actually a reason for this – as solitary animals, they had no need to develop much in the way of facial expressions and have fewer muscles in their faces with which to create them (social animals such as dogs, on the other hand, need the means to 'show' other members of their group how they feel, because they are constantly in their company). But this doesn't mean that cats aren't quite easily frightened or made apprehensive by loud noises or sudden, abrupt touch, or being picked up unexpectedly. Nor does it mean that they don't express themselves; you simply have to look more closely to spot the subtler signs. Two things that you've almost certainly noticed that your cat does when they're feeling friendly are bunting and the slow eye-blink. Bunting is a cat's almost universal practice of rubbing against things – it renders something familiar by adorning it with scent from the glands around their face. You won't be able to smell it, but your cat will, and gentle petting in response is rarely rejected. The slow eye-blink is just as it sounds, and it's a feline 'hello' – it's used between friendly cats. In 2021 a study at the University of Sussex found that a relaxed cat recognizes a slow-blink, even from a human face, so keep watch, and if your cat slow-blinks at you, make sure to slow-blink back.

ARE BREED CATS DIFFERENT?

There's a lot of anecdotal evidence that breed affects personality and a 2019 study in Finland on over 5,700 cats of nineteen different breeds also found that a cat's background does make a difference, even at a few generations removed.

Handsome is as handsome does

While the International Cat Association recognizes more than seventy distinct breeds of cat, only around 5 per cent of pet cats in the UK and the US are purebred, although many more have one breed parent or can trace a couple of generations' worth of heredity. The vast majority of recent selective breeding has been for appearance rather than personality, though without such extreme results as are found in dogs (while a Siamese looks quite different from a Persian, it's still a much less pronounced difference than that between, say, a Chihuahua and a Great Dane).

Breeding has long been thought to have some effect on the behaviour and personality of pet cats, although cats, like dogs, often suffer from breed stereotyping.

You've probably heard that Siamese cats are vocal and that Bengals are slightly wild; that Norwegian Forest Cats are especially affectionate or British Shorthairs are easy to be around, and the Finnish study proved that a lot of these preconceptions were true – to a certain extent. Whatever their upbringing and environment, some characteristics seemed to be bred into the cats they studied. Perhaps the most surprising takeaway was that 'house cats' – regular domestic moggies of no known pedigree – were found in general to be more anxious around people, less sociable and more inclined to aggression than most purebred cats. Researchers speculated that carefully bred cats may have become used to more human interaction and handling – particularly where some of the kittens would have a future as show cats – so could have become habituated to being around people.

The results of breeding

Pedigree could be worth considering If you have very specific needs. If you live in a small space, don't go for a breed that likes an outdoor life, for example. But above most inherited characteristics, the thing that makes the most difference to how comfortable an adult cat is around people is the quality and quantity of its early experiences. Look for a litter that has had plenty of gentle handling and opportunities for play.

If you want a specific breed of cat, research it before approaching a breeder. Do your homework – however beautiful or affectionate, some breeds have inherited predispositions to health conditions or other problems, so you need to know the right questions to ask.

TWENTY-FOUR HOURS

HOW CATS SPEND THEIR TIME

If it seems to you that your cat spends most of its time asleep, with a few breaks for eating and grooming, you might be quite close to the truth. But cats' bursts of activity can be just as intense, and it's often when we're asleep that they're at their most energetic.

Sleep and other adventures

In 2017 an Icelandic TV series became a sleeper hit. It was the straightforward recording of the lives of a family of four rescue kittens, with the shows taking selections from a twenty-four-hour-a-day livestream. The results showed that the habits of the individuals varied, as you'd expect, but the breakdown across a few days was fairly consistent. On average, the fit, growing cats spent sixteen hours every day sleeping. If that seems like a lot, consider this: as cats age, they sleep more, and elderly cats can clock up twenty-two hours' sleep in every twenty-four.

First-time cat owners are always surprised by how many hours' sleep a perfectly healthy cat can clock up...

...and they may be equally astonished by the ferocity and pace of a well-rested cat who's determined to play.

Although the eight hours remaining may not seem like a lot of time to enjoy a full life, the TV cats had it sorted. Two hours were taken up with grooming, while a further two were spent on observation time – that tireless watchfulness familiar to everyone who lives with a cat, whether it is carried out from an indoor windowsill or from an outdoor perch, such as a wall or the roof of a convenient shed. Two more hours were spent on territory patrol and 'adventures', mostly that night-time exploration that remains a mystery to owners, who can only guess what cats may have been up to from the clues they carry back – a scratch or two, evidence of hunting perhaps, or a feline disagreement. Territory patrol will include scent-marking and scent-collecting. How much ground a cat's territory covers varies a lot, however: town cats may patrol an area of a few back gardens, or even less if there's a big population of cats locally and they want to avoid territorial fights, but rural cats have been known to go further; fitted with monitors, some have been found to roam as far as a thousand acres of territory.

Free time

When a cat has slept, watched, explored and groomed, on average they're left with around two free hours in the day for eating, toileting and playing. Playing may be solo and impulsive, or they can be tempted into play by you, or sometimes, and if they're comfortable and familiar with each other, by another cat. The 'crazy ten minutes' that sees some cats rushing around wildly in a sudden burst of energy, often at the end of the day as it's starting to get dark, seems to be a way of using up pent-up energy that hasn't had an outlet – it's more common in indoor cats who have less opportunity to explore and wander. If it happens often, it's worth considering if you could spend more one-to-one playtime with your cat.

HOW WE KNOW WHAT WE KNOW

Cats have, perhaps unfairly, taken a back seat to dogs when it comes to behavioural research over the last two decades. But they've become more popular study subjects over the last few years, and scientists are learning more all the time.

Why dogs and not cats?

Pet cats are popular; globally, it's estimated that we keep something like three times as many pet cats as pet dogs. But even their most fervent fans would admit that they don't pander to our expectations and, historically, we've left them very much to their own devices. This fits in with their evolutionary background – they were always solitary, and joined human activity for a single, mutually beneficial reason, which has never really changed. People keep pet cats today because they are beautiful, entertaining and sometimes affectionate, but in the main they don't expect to shape their behaviour. Dogs, on the other hand, were social animals from the start, and humans have bred them selectively for hundreds of years to fulfil roles that cover everything from companion to guard, and herder to hunter, so they come with a ready prepped relationship in which they expect to cooperate with humans and are likely to want to please. At the most basic level, their behaviour and responses are easier to study than those of cats. Interviewed in 2019, one of the great pioneers in cognitive studies from the late 1990s, primarily with dogs, Ádám Miklósi of Eötvös Loránd University in Budapest, ruefully admitted that 'We know more about how wolves think.'

OPPOSITE: Dogs have always been more straightforward subjects for study than cats, but scientific interest in the latter is growing, as is the amount that we're learning.

A growing field

Miklósi has tried to study cats in the past. In 2005, he organized for cats to take part in a 'pointing test' – a classic in cognitive testing, which studies whether or not animals understand that when a person points at something, it indicates that they should look at the object being pointed at, rather than the person doing the pointing. Dogs had long been successful in passing the pointing test, but the cats' independence of mind proved to be a setback in the comparison study – they had an unfortunate tendency to wander off from the test and not return.

Things have changed quite a lot since then. More recent studies have looked at the relationships between cats and their owners and have found that cats refer to their owners for support, protection and simply to get more information in a puzzling or mildly intimidating situation. And the number of studies is growing all the time – research-wise, cats seem on the brink of becoming a popular species for the first time since modern behavioural science began.

PLAYING & ENRICHMENT

Cats are curious by nature and fascinated by many things, from a custom-made toy to a scuttling insect, or even a piece of paper rustling in a draught. Because most pet cats no longer earn their living as full-time hunters, it's important for them to have plenty of stimulation in their immediate environment – and it's up to you to provide it. A range of objects to play with and enough variation in everyday life should keep them happy and interested. The more they see you as a source of enjoyment and interest, the stronger the bond between you will become.

SPONTANEOUS GAMES

Cats are good at inventing their own entertainment – boxes or bags become dens or hides, while a leaf or feather transforms into imagined prey. And you can up the ante by creating unexpected situations, or improvising toys from everyday materials.

WHAT'S THE PAYOFF?

Cats are stimulated by surprises; swapping elements of their environment around and introducing new challenges every so often encourages them to explore and have fun in their everyday space.

Make an obstacle course

You're probably used to the extraordinary acrobatic feats that cats can achieve, climbing near-vertical surfaces and balancing on the tiniest footholds. You may also have seen the online videos in which cats are surprised by, for example, a corridor blocked by hundreds of inverted plastic cups, and enjoyed watching the ways they find to negotiate them. Make the most of a cat's enthusiasm for exploring new levels and surfaces by making them a temporary obstacle course. Pick a time when your cat isn't in the room, then take as many random objects as you can lay hands on – large books, short lengths of wood, solid cardboard boxes, a chair or two – and imagine that you're creating a jungle gym on a small scale. Make a bridge between two stable chairs with a piece of wood, for example, or pile up books so that a normally out-of-reach shelf is suddenly within range. When you've finished, test your creations for stability (you don't want your cat hurt while they're exploring) and move out of harm's way anything precious that has become newly accessible. Leave the 'course' in place for a couple of days and enjoy watching what your cat makes of it.

Bubble chasing

A very easy way to initiate a shared game is to blow bubbles for your cat. There are plenty of bubble mixes available specifically for cats, some with catnip oil for added appeal, but you really don't need anything special – provided you have a wand, a weak solution of plain washing-up liquid works perfectly well and can be mixed up on a whim. Sit or stand near to your cat, ensuring that you're in their eyeline, and blow a few bubbles for them. Soap bubbles have the advantage of drifting unpredictably, and most cats won't need much encouragement to hunt them down. Keep up a steady supply for as long as your cat's interest lasts, blowing bubbles at different levels and in different directions, ensuring that some can be pounced on and caught, while others remain enticingly out of reach until they pop.

OPPOSITE: Finish a bubble-blowing session by throwing a real toy for your cat to pounce on, so that their game doesn't end in frustration.

GROW YOUR OWN CATNIP

There's not much doubt that catnip (*Nepeta cataria*), an unremarkable-looking plant with small blue flowers, has a powerful euphoric appeal for most cats, and you can gratify the yen by growing your own.

How catnip works

If you've seen a cat being 'sent' by catnip – they look more as though they're tripping than playing – an episode of stretching, kneading, writhing and mouthing will be followed by a short break before the cat returns to the source to do it all over again. The substance that provokes this feline high is called nepetalactone – a scent molecule that's believed to bind to specific receptors in cats, which result in a direct 'hit' to the brain. The magic doesn't work on every cat – around one in three is indifferent to it – and those who don't respond have an inherited genetic difference from those who do.

Serving it up

If your cat belongs in the group that adores catnip, you can grow your own. It's cheapest grown from seed – there are lots of varieties, many colloquially called catmint or catnip, so look for the Latin name, *Nepeta cataria*, on the packet to make sure you're buying the right plant. It's a resilient crop which only needs quick-draining soil and sun to thrive, although it's best to cover

WHAT'S THE PAYOFF?

The majority of cats love catnip, and there are no ill-effects to counteract the high it produces.

new seedlings to make sure your cat's attentions don't stifle them. Once old enough and tough enough, raise the plants in the corner of a garden bed, or plant them in a large, shallow pot or tray if you're growing in a yard, or on a windowsill or balcony. An area around 30-cm (12-in) square should be large enough to give your cat the satisfaction of rolling on it as well as smelling and nibbling it.

Towards the end of summer, when the plants are larger and have flowered, cut the stems and dry the bunch of catnip by hanging it upside down – when it's thoroughly dry, crumble the leaves, stems and flowers, discarding the twiggier bits, to make a rough mixture which can be used in the same way as the tubs of dried catnip you can buy (see pages 34–5).

Can cats overdose?

Sometimes a cat's love of catnip can get a bit too intense. Don't worry – it isn't addictive and it can't harm your cat. If your pet's interest seems a little obsessive, remove the catnip toy or cover up the plant for a few days until normal service resumes.

Some cats sniff delicately, while others go in for a full-on rolling session. If your cat is a catnip roller, don't worry – the plant is resilient enough to spring back from the encounter.

CATNIP READYMADES
AND SOME OTHER OPTIONS

If you are unable to grow your own, there are lots of catnip products on the market – dried, spray-on or readymade toys that come filled with it. And if your cat is left cold by catnip, there are other options you can try which offer the same stimulation.

WHAT'S THE PAYOFF?

Catnip can be served up in different ways according to preference – and those cats who aren't susceptible can usually get the same euphoric high from one of the alternatives.

Top up stuffed toys with a handful of fresh or dried catnip every so often to keep them interesting for your cat.

Different uses

Dried catnip, whether grown or bought, can be used to fill homemade toys. If you like sewing you can get creative with your own designs; if you don't, your cat won't mind some simpler ways of getting their hit. Put a handful into an old, clean, long sock and stitch it closed – the snakey shape means that your cat can twist around its whole length, maximizing their exposure to the scent. Alternatively, slit the seam of a soft toy that your cat already likes and add some catnip before sewing it up again. If you have a cat who is keen on hard toys, use one of the lightweight treat balls that can be snapped open and refilled (they're often sold with a bag of catnip included), or stuff the centre of a hollow kong-type toy with dried leaves and stems. The effectiveness of catnip wanes over time, so replace the fillings or refresh with catnip spray regularly.

Alternative highs

There are two other options offering a similar appeal for cats who aren't interested in catnip. The first is Tatarian honeysuckle (*Lonicera tatarica*). It isn't a grow-it-yourself option – it's a shrub which grows large and woody in its native Central Asia, and its leaves, flowers and berries are all toxic – but the wood contains a scent molecule which, while different from that of catnip, has a similar effect on most cats. It's sold in various forms – carved into simple toys, or as small logs or slices of wood. The response it produces is like that elicited by catnip; and, again, its effects can fade – when that happens, spritzing the wood with water will renew its appeal.

The second choice comes from a plant called silver vine (*Actinidia polygama*). It's a member of the kiwi family, and the active ingredients are two different scent molecules – nepetalactone (found in catnip) and actinidine, which has the same kind of effect but seems to appeal to a greater number of cats. It's most commonly sold as a powder, which can be sprinkled on toys, bedding or other objects. Cat owners report that, of the three options, it seems to produce the strongest reaction of all.

CARDBOARD FOR CATS

Anyone who has ever owned a cat will be aware of the powerful charm exerted by any and every cardboard box. You can build on that appeal – literally – by collecting several boxes together and making something a bit more elaborate for your cat to enjoy.

WHAT'S THE PAYOFF?

Making cardboard-box architecture boosts your own creativity – and few cats will be able to resist the results.

Ensure that your cardboard structures are sturdy enough to hold the weight of a high-climbing cat.

High-rise or bungalow?

How fancy you want to go depends on how long you want to spend and how many boxes you've accumulated. If you're not immediately inspired, or if you're short of time, try one of these simple ideas to start with – if it's a hit with your cat, you can branch out into some more elaborate projects.

• Tunnel living

Take four or five cardboard boxes of roughly similar size and cut the tops and bottoms out so that each box becomes a tube. Cut one or two round holes of various sizes in two sides of each box, drawing round the base of a small glass, a mug and a large saucer before cutting so that they're fairly even. Then line up the boxes, each resting on an uncut side, to make a tunnel with round 'windows' in the sides. Use parcel tape to stick them together. Drape a tea towel over one of the open ends and tape it in place on the top of the box. No cat will be able to resist pulling aside the 'curtain' and wandering through the tunnel, looking out through the portholes.

• Cardboard high-rise

You will need several sturdy boxes of different sizes, but all large enough for your cat to climb inside. Leave two opposite sides of each box whole, but cut one or two holes of different sizes on the other four sides of each box. Cut one hole big enough for your cat to climb through in one side of each box. Then pile them four or five high, securing them on each side with plenty of parcel tape. Weight the bottom box with a few heavy books or cans to give the pile stability.

• Rollerball tower

A variant on the high-rise – instead of leaving the 'floor' and 'roof' of the boxes completely solid, cut holes in each base and each top, and align each pair of holes as you stick the boxes together. The end result should be that when a ball is dropped into the tower of boxes, having dropped down one floor, it will then have to run across to the next pair of holes to drop down through the next box. An interested cat, patting the ball around, will help to manoeuvre it down to the base of the tower. All the base/top holes should be small-saucer sized – that is, large enough for a table-tennis or other lightweight ball to drop through.

PACKAGING PAYOFFS

Never throw out a piece of packaging without first considering if your cat can make use of it. Cardboard boxes are great, but there are plenty of other good games to be had from all kinds of paper, card and other free materials.

Mixing textures

Cats love anything that makes a crackly noise, so save tissue and bubblewrap, along with brown paper, corrugated card, eggboxes and cardboard tubes. For the most basic game, fill a cardboard box with a range of different materials, incorporate a few loosely wrapped treats among them, then give it to your cat to explore.

Tube games

For something that lasts a little longer but is still quick to make, collect a few weeks' worth of cardboard tubes and a smallish, sturdy box (a shoebox is ideal). Cut the base out of the box, cut the tubes to match the box's depth, and fill the box 'frame' with cardboard tubes, building them up from the bottom and gluing them in place as you go. When the frame is fully packed and the glue is dry, you'll be left with something quite sturdy that looks like an outsize bug hotel. Fill the tubes with crinkly, rustling paper,

WHAT'S THE PAYOFF?

A wide range of different sorts of packaging can offer a lot of fun for a cat before, ready-shredded, they're consigned to the recycling bin.

adding treats or twists of paper full of dried catnip or a sprinkling of silver vine powder. A more elaborate version is a tube 'stockade', made from different lengths of cardboard tube glued either sideways or end-on to a larger piece of card in a semi-circle. You can pack them in the same way, leaving short ends of paper or card sticking up from the top of each tube so that your cat can pull them out to empty the tube.

Pop-up prey

If you've ever played splat the rat, you'll understand the appeal of trying to wallop a pop-up target; if anything, your cat will be even keener on the idea. For an improvised splat game, you need a box with a lid and one long side cut out (a shoebox will work well). Cut half-a-dozen holes in the top, using the base of a small glass as a template. Then make your 'rats': crumple together four or five balls of crinkly paper or bubble wrap, small enough to fit easily through the holes in the top of the box. Cut a matching number of strips of heavy card around 30cm (12in) long. Fold around 5cm (2in) of one end of each strip at a right angle to the rest of it, and use tape to fasten one of the paper balls to this shorter length. Put the box in your cat's sightline and, sitting at the back and holding two or three strips in each hand, 'pop' one at a time up through one of the holes, pulling it back as your cat moves to bat it. As your cat gets more engaged, you'll have to move fast to have several rats in play at once: good exercise for both of you.

Cardboard tubes lend themselves to both simple or elaborate structures, depending on how many you've collected and your patience level.

CASTING A LURE

The first time you played with a kitten, the game probably relied on a piece of string, maybe with a cork tied to the end, pulled jerkily along the floor. Chasing a lure is a lifelong enthusiasm for most cats, and you can offer a variety to keep them interested.

Fishing games

If your cat is already happy with a length of string and a reel or cork, you can speed up the game – and offer an even more tempting prey for them to hunt. Use a cheap toy fishing rod, from either the pet store or the toy shop, so that you can 'cast' the bait – the rod lets you 'float' the prey further away, which your cat may find more intriguing than a simple dragging action, then you can quickly reel it back in.

What should you cast? You can buy readymade 'flies', put together from bunches of fur fabric or feathers, or hook one of your cat's favourite toys to the line, or even scent a small stuffed toy or ball with catnip or silver pine to give the game extra oomph. Small fish toys containing sensors are also available – they wriggle in a lifelike way when touched and, used with a line, give most cats an energy burst as they leap to 'land' them.

When you've chosen what's on the end of the line and made your first cast, vary the pace of the lure and the level at which it's held. You'll find that when it comes briefly to a halt, your cat may freeze and start to slow-stalk it, only to resume a full-on chase as it skitters away again. Run it along the floor then have it rise above your cat's head level to make the game acrobatic, too. You might also sometimes leave it to be discovered – trail it across a doorway or from the back of a chair or sofa, so that the cat has a surprise glimpse of it, or leave the lure concealed under a cushion or throw or mat, so that it can spring into motion when your cat's passing by.

OPPOSITE: Use a range of toys with the lure; a surprise element will help to keep up your cat's interest levels.

KEEP IT SAFE

Cats get very engrossed when playing with lures, so make sure there's no opportunity for your pet to swallow a length of the string. Don't use wool, which is too easily bitten through; instead, use strong string, thin tape or nylon line. When the game is over, don't leave it lying around; wind it up and put it out of the way in a closed drawer.

WHAT'S THE PAYOFF?

Regular lively games with a lure are good exercise for your cat; make sure you let them 'win' every so often – that is, capture the prize – so that they don't lose interest.

MOBILE ENTERTAINMENT

Mobiles have all the qualities to appeal to a cat – moving things to watch, enticing just-out-of-reach possibilities for acrobatic jumping, and – if you make your own and include plenty of different ingredients – lots of variety of texture, and even taste.

Make your own

You'll find every imaginable variation on mobiles with which to entertain your cat – there are even versions for kittens that mimic a human baby's activity mat. If you make your own basic version, though, you can deconstruct and reinvent it whenever you want to keep your cat's interest going – and you also won't be adding to the global pile of plastic waste.

Start with a metal or wooden frame to hang it from – you can make this from a couple of metal clothes hangers, unwound and re-bent into a rough circle, or two or three bendy wooden plant supports, bent into a curve, overlapped to make an oval shape, and bound in place with tape. Suspend it from a string tied to either side of the frame and then hung from a hook from a window frame, a door or the ceiling. To add the interesting bits, use different lengths of tough string, one end tied firmly to the frame and the other to a woollen pompom, a small bunch of feathers, grass or dried catnip, pieces of raffia, and so on. You can include some of your cat's favourite biscuit treats, too, either tied on directly if they're large enough, or contained in a small hollow ball that can be opened up when it's 'caught'. When you've got a sufficiently intriguing range of objects, hang up the mobile. Try to place it so it catches the draught, as the movement will increase its appeal to your cat.

Don't forget that cats are highly attuned to sounds as well as to movement and may appreciate some noise elements in a homemade mobile, so an alternative option is to customize a regular wind chime with some of the strings described above.

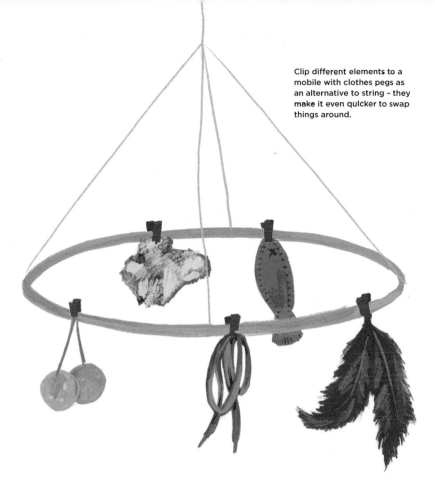

Clip different elements to a mobile with clothes pegs as an alternative to string – they make it even quicker to swap things around.

Hang it right

Whichever option you go for, the mobile should be hung securely at the right height – so that it's hard but not impossible for your cat to reach high enough to 'catch' one of the strings. When they do, the hook that holds it must be strong enough to ensure the whole mobile doesn't come down. Watch your cat as they play, and adjust the mobile's height if necessary.

WHAT'S THE PAYOFF?

Mobiles are low-maintenance entertainment for your cat; change one or two elements every so often, or shift the whole mobile to a new location to reignite your pet's interest.

TUNNEL GAMES

Toy tunnels are more often associated with dogs than cats, due to their use in canine agility courses. A small, light toy tunnel, though, can become a cat favourite, offering both a good hiding place and an excellent spot from which to stage an ambush.

What type of tunnel?

The simplest, single-channel collapsible play tunnel made from nylon fabric held up with rigid rings is probably the best value long-term. Not only does it flatten into a disc so that it's easy to store (important, unless you have a dedicated cat playroom), but it's also easier to move around to different spots than some of the other heftier options on the market, which may come in fur fabric, or take a more complicated 'maze' form with several arms – fun to play with, but bulky and harder to clean. It's worth looking for a tunnel with lookout holes in the sides and top, though, as most cats will enjoy taking quick, covert glances out of the enclosed space. If you have a choice, pick a longer tunnel (4m/13ft, or so) to maximize the play possibilities – some shorter options can be fastened together to make a double length, too.

What do cats like about tunnels? First and foremost, a tunnel gives them a private space that's good both to hide in and as an observation spot. The thin nylon fabric also makes a rustling noise when it's moved, which will appeal to most cats. They can be used both indoors and out; when outdoors, use small stones to weight the ends of a very lightweight tunnel to keep it in place and secure: cats are sometimes reluctant to use something that looks insecure.

OPPOSITE: The open end of a play tunnel may be added to your cat's list of useful lookout stations around the house and garden.

Ways to play

Most of the games you play with your cat will be improved by a tunnel. You can drag a lure past the opening to encourage an ambush from your cat, or roll a ball, or more excitingly, set off a wind-up toy to run through it, prompting a rushed pursuit. You can dust the inside with catnip, which may result in an ecstatic in-tunnel reverie, or use it to set the start of a treat trail, laying three or four treats along the length of the tunnel, then hiding more beyond its far end, concealed around the room (or, if you're outside, in the garden). You may find that your cat even opts to sleep in their tunnel, using it as a safe space in which to hide away.

WHAT'S THE PAYOFF?

As far as a cat is concerned, a toy tunnel offers all the charm of a cardboard box – and it's likely to last much longer, too.

NOW YOU SEE IT...

You may already have spotted – and possibly rejected – the gloves with spookily elongated fingers, sometimes complete with pompoms, that are sold in pet shops. Not so fast: they're actually an excellent (and safe) means of playing up close with your cat.

Hand-to-paw play

Playing with your cat bare-handed and up close always comes with the associated risk of getting scratched, so while these gloves might look eccentric, they make an excellent addition to the toy collection. Think of them as lightweight armour for your hands! Introduce them gently if your cat's new to them – first, leave them around so they can be sniffed at and examined, then put them on but keep your hands still and encourage your cat to take a closer look. When you do start to play, use the long fingers to softly pat and push, rather than to poke and probe, so that your cat can engage with them easily and without becoming intimidated. If their claws do come out, softly push the glove closer into your cat's body rather than sharply pulling away. Although this may seem counter-intuitive, it's the opposite of what real prey would do, and because the glove isn't 'struggling to get away', your cat is actually more likely to release their grip – after all, the point of the gloves is to avoid being scratched yourself, rather than to encourage your cat to be more combative.

Branching out

Add strings with other playthings tied to the ends of the fingers to create lures and trail them along – because they're actually attached to your hands, it's easier to control where they go, as your cat, intrigued, starts to follow. Then hold your hands up high to make a temporary mobile which demands some stretching and jumping to reach. Alternatively, use the glove to make an ambush – push it, with your hand in it, under a rug or leave the fingers sticking out from under a piece of furniture, then make it dart out as your cat passes, to provoke a chase.

KEEP THEM SAFE

Check over the gloves before playing – the fingers are often reinforced with plastic or wire struts with sharp ends, which, over time and with plenty of use, can push through the fabric.

WHAT'S THE PAYOFF?

Long-fingered gloves let you play at your cat's pace without worrying about those lightning-quick changes of feline mood which can result in scratches when the game intensifies.

Even though it can be tempting to play more boldly when you can't be scratched, keep things gentle when you're wearing gloves.

POOL BOBBING

If your cat prefers to drink from a dripping tap or to reach an experimental paw into the bathtub (while you're in it), they might enjoy some more creative use of water. Even those who are less keen may eventually enjoy a water game or garden fountain.

WHAT'S THE PAYOFF?

Cats can cool off in hot weather by playing with water, and the rippling movement of a new element is great for holding their attention.

Reflections and movement

Water probably appeals because it combines the patterns of light and movement that are so engrossing for cats with an intriguingly different sensation if they feel or pat its surface. There's also a school of thought that believes that cats are attracted to moving water instinctively because it tends to be safer to drink than still – and therefore potentially stagnant – pools, and, because their close-up vision isn't very strong, they 'pat' to see if there's any current. The simplest water toy you can make is a large plastic plant saucer or shallow bowl filled with water, with various objects floating in it. Try ping-pong balls, pieces of paper (small origami boats are great because they're light enough to push across the water easily, and surprisingly hard to sink) – or use small natural objects such as twigs and leaves, which can be gently pushed around. A few cat biscuits can supply a floating snack (remove them before they get too soggy if your cat isn't keen – not every cat likes 'fishing' for their food).

Safety around water

Contrary to traditional lore, most cats can swim and a handful may even enjoy it, but the majority prefer not to immerse themselves in water. If you have any deepish water in your garden, though, net it off, as ponds can be a strong hunting draw for cats and they can easily fall in.

Cat fountains

A cat that loves a tap might like their own water fountain. There are numerous versions available online and from almost every pet shop, from the inexpensive to the quite luxurious, but they're generally designed first and foremost for drinking from, rather than for play. An alternative is a small solar-powered water fountain that can be floated on a water pool outside – you can use anything from a very large plastic plant saucer to a low bird bath as a container – and which is light enough to be pushed by a paw. The solar aspect means that it operates infrequently, so it also offers a welcome surprise element as far as your cat is concerned – now you see a jet of water, now you don't!

OPPOSITE: Vary what you offer as floats in a bobbing game, from ping-pong balls to twigs or pieces of apple.

A ROOM WITH A VIEW

Cats love a window perch. Not all views are equal, though; while many will happily watch passers-by, their favourite outlook is a green view – trees and plants with all their variety of natural movement, as well as tempting glimpses of birds and squirrels.

Window life

Whether it's urban or bucolic, your cat will usually take full advantage of any view. Make it easy for them and clear windowsills (and any surfaces that might be used as jumping points en route) of anything breakable, and add a cushion or rug for added comfort. If there isn't a sill, set up a perch at a similar height – a small, sturdy, uncluttered table that's of a height to be jumped up on should work fine.

Screen time for cats

What if you don't have any kind of natural view to offer? One possibility is cat TV – not aimed at you, but rather video that's put together with the aim of appealing *to* cats. Special programmes, featuring a range of bird, rodent and fish life going about its business, have been available for the last decade plus; whether or not they're a good thing divides both cat owners and cats. For every feline fan, there's a cat who really isn't interested in anything that takes place on a screen; at the other end of the scale, some owners worry about their cats becoming overly focused on watching wildlife that can't be hunted and which doesn't, in cat terms, really exist.

If you think your cat might be a fan, judge their reaction to a regular wildlife programme before getting them the cat version. Mostly what they'll be seeing is different sorts and speeds of movement – cats see movement in more detail than we do, and still scenes in rather less – and if they don't show interest in a documentary about life in the tropical rainforest, they're unlikely to react favourably to a more tailor-made film of bird feeders and their visitors. On the other hand, if your cat is interested enough to watch, but doesn't try to interact directly with the life on screen, cat TV may offer them an enjoyable alternative to a more mundane window view.

WHAT'S THE PAYOFF?

Cats evolved as sit-and-wait hunters, and your pet can be kept happily occupied for hours simply watching the world go by, provided they've got a safe and comfortable perch.

OPPOSITE: For your cat, every view offers a world full of minute variety and movement, especially if you can offer them a green landscape to gaze out on.

STAYING FIT & WELL

Looking at your cat, spread out in their usual deep doze in one of the half-dozen spots they favour, you'd be forgiven for thinking that feline wellbeing seems to come naturally. The previous chapter looked at ways you can play with your cat; this one looks at types of stimulation and interest you can offer, from providing plenty of places to sharpen their claws to raising their energy levels with laser play and making sure they have hidey holes to retreat to when needed. Cats do best when they're treated like the clever, curious creatures they are, rather than pets that don't need too much engagement.

INDOOR OR OUTDOOR CAT?

Many more cats live exclusively indoor lives now than in the past. If this is your cat, they will need to have plenty of activities to occupy them, and ideally plenty of direct interaction with you, too, to compensate for the lack of the stimulation of the outdoors.

Avoiding boredom

There are various reasons why a cat may need to be kept indoors. Sometimes they live in places where it's just too dangerous to allow them to roam – too close to a main road, for example. Sometimes the issue is that their owners don't want them to hunt or to get into territorial rows with other cats. Whatever the reason, if you have an indoor cat, make sure they're given the chance to express natural behaviours. This means:

• somewhere to scratch (while outdoor cats usually enjoy scratching posts and other scratching paraphernalia inside, they also use trees and fences outside, indoor cats depend only on what you provide);
• high-up perches where they can feel secure;
• plenty of places to hide away when they need privacy and, where possible, a view of the outside for stimulation.

Playtime may be especially important to an indoor cat, so set aside three or four dedicated breaks of ten or fifteen minutes every day to engage with your pet and play different games with them, including energetic laser or wand games to use up some of their energy.

Indoor/outdoor spaces

If you have some outdoor space that could be enclosed to make a safe area for your indoor cat, consider it – it may be easier (and cheaper) to make than you expect, and most cats thoroughly enjoy the scents of the outdoors, even if they can't roam far. Given the rather twee name of 'catios', these enclosures are already very popular in North America, and are becoming increasingly familiar in the UK and parts of Europe. They range from basic constructions made from wood and chicken wire, with a cat perch or two inside, and perhaps a wooden 'bridge' between them, to cat palaces that include somewhere for the owner to sit as well as multiple perches, hammocks and other luxurious options for the cat. They're available in flat-pack form at a range of price points, but if you're good at making things you can probably create your own; homemade versions often have a Heath Robinson charm that the ones you can buy can't match.

OPPOSITE: An indoor/outdoor contained space for your cat needs to be sturdy and safe, but a simple version can be homemade if you have basic DIY skills.

THE JOY OF SCRATCHING

It's natural behaviour for cats to scratch – which isn't much comfort when their preferred surface is the arm of your ancient (or worse, brand-new) and loved sofa. There are ways to redirect scratching, though, with a scratching pole being the most popular.

Scratching keeps a cat's claws in shape and is an opportunity for them to lay down their scent from the glands between their paw pads. Cats also seem to enjoy a luxuriant stretch-out as they scratch. Cats tend to remain faithful to scratching posts, so if you can redirect your pet's scratching in the first place, the chances are good that they'll settle for their new spot.

WHAT'S THE PAYOFF?

Accommodate your pet's need to scratch by trying a few options until you find the one that suits your cat (and saves your furniture).

If you'd prefer your cat not to go for the furniture, try offering something more appealing to their tastes.

The dos and don'ts of scratching posts

People sometimes complain that they bought a scratching post but their cat won't use it. Check the following points carefully and make sure any post you consider meets your cat's criteria. Think, too, about where you put it.

• **It must be sturdy and on a solid base.**
A rocky or unstable post will scare your cat.

• **It should be tall enough to let your cat scratch at full stretch.**
Allow at least 1m (3ft) from the base; higher won't hurt.

• **It must be covered in something appealing.**
Some research has indicated that most cats prefer a fairly loose-woven covering with a vertical weave, and the more torn and ragged it became, the more they seemed to like it. This is the texture that allows them a satisfying scratch without catching or jagging their claws. Many cat trees are covered with sisal, tightly wound round the pole, which is a hit with some cats, but which others don't take to; if you've had a failure with sisal, seek out something with a looser texture which your cat may prefer.

(Generally, the study showed that they didn't like very tight-woven, woolly fabric, so this may be the answer to your scratched sofa: while your cat is being redirected to a scratching post, tightly cover the surface you *don't* want scratched with a piece of dense, bobbly fabric, such as thick tweed.)

• **It should be in an 'important' area of the house.**
This should preferably be in a visible and walked-through spot (possibly even next door to the furniture that's already scratched). A scratching post probably won't be the most aesthetically pleasing thing in your house, but because your cat is leaving their mark, they may like to scratch somewhere obvious, on a main path; if you tuck the post in a corner, it might remain unused. Once it's been established and well-loved, you could try relocating it to a slightly less prominent spot.

MORE JOYS OF SCRATCHING

If you have a cat who is a very keen scratching enthusiast, you may find that one scratching post is not enough; they'll engage with various 'scratchers' with different surfaces and in different locations. You may even want to make some alternatives yourself.

Make your own tree-stump scratcher

This is an easy project, although it calls for a lot of corrugated card. Carefully made, it'll have more visual appeal than your average scratching post, though it's unlikely to enjoy anything like its longevity. Many cats love the fact that it's both a perch and a satisfying scratching option.

Outdoor cats grow up scratching on wood, and a cardboard stump pays tribute to this heritage. You need a big roll of corrugated card and a large tube of very strong glue. You're going to make an authentically irregular-looking tree stump by layering up cardboard.

1. Cut two templates out of newspaper – the first for the bottom of the stump and the second, much smaller, but still big enough for your cat to sit on, for the top. Make the bottom template a wavy, irregular shape.

2. Cut successive layers of corrugated card, each one a little smaller than the lowest one, glueing them together as you go, and changing the shape as it gains height, until the top few layers match the size and shape of the top template. Aim for at least 80cm (32in) in height.

3. When it's done, and the glue is dry, scatter a little catnip on the top.

Corrugated card is scratching catnip for many cats: a constructed 'tree stump' made from it offers your pet a perch as well as somewhere to scratch.

Floor and doorframe options

A few cats prefer to scratch on a horizontal surface (and plenty of others will use both vertical and horizontal scratchers). You can buy flat frames with scratching material fixed to them – often sisal, or rough carpet – although it would be easy enough to make your own, using any material that seems to appeal to your cat.

If your pet likes to scratch doorframes, consider fixing a strip of carpet or other tough material around the edge of the frame and see if they are happy to scratch the alternative material instead.

WHAT'S THE PAYOFF?

Offer a few different options for a keen cat to scratch on, and vary the textures and materials so they can use the scratcher that suits their mood.

DECLAWING

If you ever hear declawing mentioned as a cure for scratching, dismiss it out of hand. It's illegal in a number of countries, including the UK, but sadly not everywhere. For those that don't know what it means, it's an operation intended to stop a cat scratching – despite the rather innocuous-sounding name, it involves the amputation of the top joints of a cat's toes. Any cat lover would consider it inhumane.

CAT TREES
PROS AND CONS

Cat trees come in myriad forms, from single trunks with one or two platforms, just about large enough for a cat to sit on, to elaborate entertainment centres incorporating built-in scratching posts and cabins, mobiles for batting at and mirrors for gazing in.

There are two schools of thought about cat trees, depending on whether concern for your cat's fun trumps concern for your décor. It's undeniable that cat trees are ugly to look at; many mainstream, inexpensive versions are quite tacky in construction and 'finished' with cheap carpet, often in beige or brown. This probably won't trouble your cat, who is more likely to be charmed by the choice of high-up perches, the appealing little huts to hide in, the handily sited scratching post, and so on, but if you've spent time arranging your living space to be pleasing to the (human) eye, you may not be able to forget, or forgive, the cat tree's appearance, however much your cat is enjoying it.

Tailored trees

Don't buy a cat tree but then decide, after your cat has fallen in love with it, that you're unable to live with it after all. If you have the space and your cat is an enthusiastic explorer who you think would enjoy a tree, look at one of two alternatives:

1. Shop around to find something that will suit your house as well as your cat, assuming that it's a long-term investment. There are styles to fit most interiors, including architectural-looking stacks of brightly coloured perches, and trees that look like actual trees, complete with realistic foliage, but the nicest examples come at a price.

2. More work, but possibly more fun – design your own and build it yourself if your skills are up to it, or find a local carpenter to put it together for you.

OPPOSITE: There are almost as many designs for cat trees as there are cats, so it's worth researching your pet's likely tastes before you buy one.

Even the heaviest cats don't weigh a huge amount, so it's possible to wall-mount huts, hammocks and platforms in a way that looks good and doesn't need too much in the way of hefty supports. If you do try this, test the weight-bearing capacity of any high-up perches with a few hefty books before you let your cat loose on them. Wall-mounting also means that you can integrate a cat space with other elements, such as bookshelves.

WHAT'S THE PAYOFF?

The right cat tree can make a cat very happy, but pick one that you, as well as your cat, can live with in the long term.

EXERCISE WITH LASERS

Laser play has plenty of plus points when it comes to energizing your cat. Lasers can be moved in ways that flutter and scuttle realistically, and few cats can resist them. But they've also come in for criticism from behaviour experts, so are they safe to use?

Point and shoot

Laser pointers have always been popular to tempt a cat to chase and pounce – they can be especially effective when you stage a game at twilight, your cat's natural hunting time. But a few concerns have been raised. First was the safety worry – the focused beam of a laser, shone directly into a cat's eyes, has the capacity to burn and damage their sight, so lasers should always be used cautiously. The nature of the game usually means that the beam runs away from your cat, rather than towards it; you should also choose a pointer with a low-power output – labelled 5mw – and, however exciting the game gets, take care where you're directing the beam.

Allowing a catch

The other worry raised around the use of lasers was whether they were good for cats psychologically. The concern was that cats, endlessly teased with a dancing beam to catch, would pounce, frequently and accurately, and repeatedly find that there was nothing under their paws. Unable to understand it, and without the satisfaction of a 'kill', the result would be frustration – and if that caused the redirection of claws and teeth onto the nearest moving objects, often human hands or feet, the game would end unhappily on both sides. If your cat seems to be becoming baffled by a laser, then arrange a pay-off at the end of each game (see opposite).

Whether or not cats find lasers ultimately frustrating probably depends on the cat. Some become passionately invested in their games, others appear to enjoy them thoroughly but still wander off when they've had enough. Limiting the time you play to around ten minutes per session should keep it fun for both sides.

GOOD LASER PLAY

- **Use the laser as it starts to get dark.**
  This is your cat's natural wake-up-and-hunt time.

- **Move the laser like prey.**
  Make brief flutters above the ground, moments of stillness as the bird 'perches', or move the laser like a mouse, sticking to the floor, but in short, scuttling rushes, and with sudden changes of direction.

- **Stay aware of where you're pointing the laser.**
  As the pace of the game picks up, take care to keep it out of your pet's eyes.

- **Keep a small motion-activated toy at hand for when you want to finish the game.** Put it on the floor and direct the laser towards it. As the cat pounces on it, it will start to wriggle; as you turn the laser off, your cat is left with the satisfaction of a catch.

WHAT'S THE PAYOFF?

Used carefully, playing with a laser can give your cat a good workout; just make sure you end the game with a win for your pet.

Vary laser play with other games, particularly if your cat tends to have an obsessive streak when playing.

PRIVACY

When it comes to your pet's need for privacy, sometimes you have to let them choose. However many safe spots you 'suggest' to your cat, the chances are that they will select their own.

Finding the right spot

Just as cats developed into hunters over millennia, so they also evolved as the prey of larger animals. Even though they no longer live in circumstances where that's likely to happen, the need to stay safe and hide away still appears to be deeply engrained. The ideal hiding spot for a cat tends to have some constant features:

1. It needs to be a tight fit. Roomy spaces don't seem to reassure cats, and every owner who has ever found their pet squeezed into a small shoebox or carrier bag knows that cats can fit into extraordinarily tiny spots.

2. It's likely to be either high up, or very close to the ground. Gaps under cupboards and beds are popular, as are the spaces above wardrobes or bookshelves. All of these are mostly used as watching spots; hiding places for rest are more likely to be somewhere cosy: airing or boiler cupboards, or the least-used sweater shelf in the wardrobe.

Leave them be

Don't ever turf a cat out of a spot they've chosen. If it's really inconvenient (after all, that comfortable drawer is going to have to be shut sometime), then wait until they've left and make it inaccessible. If they're in spots where shedding is a problem, such as a wardrobe shelf, line it with a blanket or rug that's been part of their own bedding, so they have the added bonus of their own scent, and your possessions are protected. The same goes for places that they like, but that look uncomfortable to you – add a rug or even a heating pad to that favoured under-the-bed spot to make it even cosier.

OPPOSITE: If your cat has self-selected a private space, help to make it especially comfortable with a favourite blanket or cover.

WHAT'S THE PAYOFF?

Allow your cat to pick their own hiding spots around the house, and then help them to be comfortable when they've made their choice.

The bigger picture

Why does this matter? Because there's evidence that many cats are more fearful than the people living around them think, and the single best thing that you can do for your pet is to encourage them to have trust in you. This doesn't mean invariably letting them have their own way, but it's important to respect and indulge their natural behaviours when you can.

GREEN YOUR SURROUNDINGS

Cats love greenery, indoors as well as out. They'll use large houseplants as lurking spots, and will play with them and even snack on them, getting a sensory buzz from the process. Many houseplants are toxic to cats, however, so choose carefully.

Living greenery

If you love houseplants, good news: your cat does, too. To ensure that plants and cats can live safely side by side, though, you have to take a few basic precautions. First, check and double check the species to ensure that you're not buying anything harmful to your cat. Smaller plants may need to be protected from shredding claws until they've grown large enough to survive a cat's curiosity. If you can afford it, you may find it more satisfactory to buy larger specimens in the first place, and pot them up in heavy, ceramic pots so they can't be upset by a cat's weight if your pet decides to conduct an up-close examination of the new arrivals. Grouped plants will give a jungle effect – especially pleasing to cats, who can weave among them.

Houseplants that are safe for cats include banana palms, Boston fern, areca and date palms, and that tough old stalwart of the neglectful gardener, the spider plant. Grow a spider plant spilling out of a hanging basket, suspended from a strong hook, and your cat will probably enjoy pawing and batting at the small spider-plant offspring that will soon be cascading down from the parent.

Edibles: herbs and grass

If you keep potted herbs on your kitchen windowsill, you may have noticed that your cat enjoys patting, sniffing and even occasionally chewing on a leaf or two. (Chives are to be avoided, though, as they can make cats sick, so if you grow them, keep them out of reach.)

OPPOSITE: Cats often sample the leaves of interesting plants, so ensure that anything you bring indoors is safe.

Add a container of grass, grown especially for your cat, and they're likely to be even more enthusiastic. You can buy ready-grown pots or trays of 'cat grass' from pet stores, but it's just as easy – and cheaper – to grow your own, and it will probably be lusher, too. Packets of oat, barley or wheat grass are all available, ready to be sown directly into a pot, in the same way as you grow catnip (see pages 32–3). These grasses won't have the same trippy effect on cats as catnip, but they like to sniff at and nibble on them, and they remain interesting – you'll probably see your cat returning to the pot often. As a potful grows tired, you can empty it out and sow again, alternating the different grasses to see if your cat has a favourite flavour.

WHAT'S THE PAYOFF?

Cats enjoy being around plants – bring the outdoors inside to give them their own miniature jungle to play in.

LITTER MATTERS

If you have a cat who spends a lot of time outdoors and manages all their elimination (putting it politely) out there, lucky you. For the less-fortunate majority, the litter box is simply a fact of life, and one that needs to be maintained so that you're both happy.

What your cat thinks

From your cat's point of view, probably the most important thing is that their litter box is big enough. One size doesn't necessarily fit all – while a small cat may happily use a smaller box, you'll need to size up for a larger cat, so that they can perch comfortably and go through the ritual scratch afterwards without hitting a plastic wall or scattering litter around.

It also needs to be the right height to allow for a reasonable depth of litter; ideally at least a 10-cm (4-in) layer. Elderly cats with mobility issues sometimes need a lower sill on one side of the box so they can climb in and out easily, and if you live somewhere with more than one floor, you may find that one box on each floor of the house helps to avoid accidents.

What about the litter itself? From your cat's point of view, finer-textured litters seem to be preferred to coarser ones – closer to sand than gravel. There seems to be a slight preference, too, for the unscented varieties.

Most important, if you want a contented user, keep the litter box scrupulously clean, and sited somewhere quiet and private. And if you have more than one cat, you'll likely need more than one box – many cats aren't comfortable sharing.

OPPOSITE: Keep it simple: a large, plain box, filled with a deep-enough layer of litter, stands the best chance of being popular.

What you think

As an owner, destined to scoop and clean up, you'll probably want to go for a clumping litter: it makes scooping easier and avoids that nasty drenched layer at the bottom of the box. It also means that you don't need to use a liner. How often should you clean out a box? You should scoop at least once daily, and change the litter completely every four or five days. Cats don't like (and sometimes opt not to use) dirty litter boxes, so it's in everyone's interests to keep things clean.

What about lidded boxes? In terms of cat preference, there's no evidence that the users favour them; provided the litter box is in a quiet, discreet corner, it shouldn't need a lid. The 'roof' also stops the litter drying out and can trap smells – making it less pleasant for a cat to use.

WHAT'S THE PAYOFF?

Maintain their litter box properly, keep it in a suitably calm spot and your cat should be happy to use it.

LOOKING AFTER YOUR CAT'S MOUTH

If your cat came to you as an adult, the idea that you can do anything to keep their teeth healthy may be slightly surprising. But one of the most common problems for cats – and not just the older ones – is gum and tooth infection.

Brush regularly

You brush your own teeth, but brushing your cat's is still a far from universal habit. Dental diseases afflict an estimated nine out of ten cats, however, and not only is it painful but it can also mean a lot of expensive vet visits. A cat with bad teeth and gums isn't great to be around breath-wise either. If you can begin a tooth-brushing regime when your pet is still a kitten, they'll be habituated by the time they're adults, but it may take some time and patience to get a grown-up cat used to the idea.

• **You can buy toothbrushes for cats**, but if your cat isn't keen on the idea, finger brushes (like thimbles, but with soft rubber or silicone bristles) are an easier option. You'll sometimes see cotton buds recommended; don't use them – it's too easy for a cat to panic, bite the end off, and swallow it.

• **Use cat toothpaste, never the human variety**. The latter may contain xylitol, which is toxic to cats.

• **Build up to the actual brushing over a week or two**, keeping everything very slow and gentle. Begin by letting your cat sniff the open toothpaste. Then put a small amount onto a finger brush and let your cat sniff it. After two or three sessions of sniff-the-toothpaste, choose a moment when your cat is relaxed to raise their top lip and dab a little paste on their teeth. Carry on like this, taking baby steps, until you're able to rub toothpaste along the teeth, paying particular attention to the join between teeth and gums, where infections tend to start. When you reach this stage, maintain it, brushing your cat's teeth – just for a minute or so – every day.

Supplements

Among the huge range of supplements available for cats are some very effective preparations to get rid of the bacteria that let plaque build up on your pet's teeth. Many are based on the enzymes found in seaweed (enthusiasts claim that seaweed also benefits gut health). Some come in the form of a combined supplement containing ingredients for other conditions; others are only for use against plaque. Most come as a powder which can be added directly to your pet's meals. Do check in with the vet before giving your cat any supplements – very few are suitable for absolutely every cat.

WHAT'S THE PAYOFF?

If you make the effort to brush your cat's teeth and give them an anti-plaque supplement in their food, they're less likely to have gum infections and teeth problems as they age.

Start a toothcare regime in kittenhood if you can – that way, it'll be painless to keep up with your adult cat.

MAKING VET VISITS EASIER

Few cats enjoy visits to the vet, and some hate it so much that their owners do their best to avoid them altogether. But regular check-ups are important, even when there isn't an immediate health problem, so how can you reduce the pain of the experience?

In advance

To get a cat to the vet, you need a carrier – and if the carrier is already a familiar element in your cat's life, it's less likely to be viewed with fear or suspicion. Keep the cat carrier open, in a quiet corner, and line it with something comfortable. Every so often, leave a treat nearby, and a couple inside. If it's inviting, your cat may well take to resting in it – and once they regard it as a safe space, making a journey in it will prove less traumatic.

Five practical steps for a visit

1. Get a half-and-half pet carrier – you can lift the deep top half off, so that your vet will be able to give your cat a preliminary check without the added stress of having to lift them out onto the table.

2. Choose the right size of carrier – too large, and your cat may slip around en route; too small, and they'll feel scarily cramped. It should be a good fit, but not too tight.

3. Line the carrier with a towel or blanket that your cat regularly rests on. It will smell familiar, which may be comforting on the journey.

4. Take an extra towel or blanket too, in case your cat pees or messes on the outward journey. It means you can at least offer a clean carrier for the return journey.

5. If you can, make an appointment which allows you to go straight in to see the vet. If you have to spend time in the waiting room, put the cat carrier up on the seat, and face it towards you and away from any other animals that are waiting.

Cats vs dogs

Statistics show that dogs are far more likely to be taken to the vet than cats. This may be because cats have the reputation of being low-maintenance pets (perhaps because it may be harder to spot the signs of pain in a cat). Keep an eye on your cat. Any major changes of habit call for a vet visit.

WHAT'S THE PAYOFF?

Keeping your cat calm during vet visits is something you have to prep for in advance, but it's worth the effort to take some of the stress out of the inevitable.

Some careful prep can reduce at least some of the stress – both for you and your cat when visiting the vet.

EATING

Compared with us, cats are highly specialized eaters – they need a mostly meat diet without much padding and they have fairly specific nutritional needs. So the reputation that cats have for being fussy is probably due more to their instinctive knowledge of these needs than to any especially rarefied approach to their food.

While not many people will want to take on the job of cooking their cat's food from scratch, it's worth learning about what your pet needs nutrition-wise, and why. You'll then be able to choose the best commercial food you can afford, and it will help you tailor-make occasional home-cooked meals or treats to enliven your pet's day-to-day diet.

SET-UP FOR GOOD EATING

Before looking at what you feed your cat, look at where you feed them. Cats need to feel safe to eat comfortably, and most remain alert to what's going on around them while they're having their meal. A secure set-up for your cat will make mealtimes serene.

Smells good, tastes good

Your cat's sensitivities are at their most acute when it comes to smell and noise, so where you feed them matters. A utility room or out-of-the-way corner of the kitchen might seem ideal until you notice all the noises that erupt unexpectedly there – in particular dishwashers and washing machines switching on and off during their programme cycles; you may not be conscious of them, but chances are your cat will find the sudden sounds stressful. Even worse is when the eating space is part of an area dedicated to 'all things cat', and their litter box is kept nearby. This is definitely one to avoid; in nature, cats go some way away to toilet, but indoors the proximity to their feeding spot will at the very least make them uneasy. Bear in mind, too, that the best eating place will be one from which your cat has a good all-round view of anyone or anything approaching. If you think the designated food station isn't as good as it could be, find a quieter corner where your pet can eat in peace.

What kind of bowl?

Go for a wide-based, shallow china or metal bowl that's broad enough to accommodate the width of your cat's whiskers and heavy enough not to slide around on the floor – metal pet bowls often have rubber rims around the base to keep them stable. Plastic may be too lightweight – if it slips about, it will feel unstable and be off-putting for your cat. Wash the bowl between meals, even if your pet eats dried food, and make sure that all traces of soap are rinsed off; the sensitive nose of a cat will sniff out – and dislike – residual smells.

Drinking matters

Cats often have strong opinions about what they will (or won't) drink from, hence the wide range of drinking fountains that you'll find for them online. The do-it-yourself version of this is the dripping tap; if this is what your cat favours, they may sit mewing in the sink until you appear to do the honours. The driving force behind this (see pages 48–9) is probably the instinctive desire to drink from running rather than still water; it may be the same impulse that leads some cats to splash around in their water bowls rather than using them to drink from. Although this can be exasperating, putting all bowls on an absorbent mat should avoid too much mess; if your cat seems to do more paddling than drinking, however, they may be a suitable candidate for a drinking fountain.

WHAT'S THE PAYOFF?

A cat who feels secure in the knowledge that their meals will be served up in a quiet corner where they don't have to watch their back will be able to get the most out of their food.

An ideal feeding station has a good view of its surroundings, so that your cat feels safe while eating.

HOW CATS EAT WELL

Cats need meat – even if you're a vegetarian, there is no healthy way for your cat to follow suit. In the wild, their prey is usually eaten as soon as it's caught, and isn't supplemented with much else. This means that cats are not suited to a very mixed diet.

Runs on meat

Every species has an ideal diet that its system has evolved to digest and on which it can thrive. Your cat is no exception; they're what's known as an obligate carnivore, which means that they're meat-fuelled. They eat meat not through choice (in the way that your dog might prefer a nice steak to a balanced chicken-veg-rice meal, say) but through necessity – because it contains substances they need, in a form that their body can use and that can't be found in most other foods.

First, there are the amino acids. There are eleven of these that a cat's system can't make for itself; the two most important are taurine and arginine. If they don't get enough taurine, cats can suffer from heart and eye problems; inadequate arginine can result in ammonia poisoning. Second are the vitamins. Unlike humans, cats can't manufacture vitamin A or enough vitamin D themselves to stay healthy. Both the amino acids and the vitamins are found in absorbable, usable form in meat.

It's complicated

A good cat food is made up mostly of meat (or fish, of which more on page 83). Most commercial food is cooked, and because cooking can degrade some substances, more may be added later (commercial cat food, for example, usually has extra taurine added after cooking). Commercial food also inevitably contains ingredients that cats wouldn't get in the wild, where they'd eat small mammals and birds rather than the beef, chicken, lamb and fish that feature in shop-bought 'menus' – but the important thing the ingredients have in common is that they contain animal protein and thus the key elements to keep cats well.

Cats also need a diet relatively rich in animal fats – vegetable fats won't do the job – both for the fatty acids they contain and to help them absorb fat-soluble vitamins. This is one of the reasons that dogs are often more interested in cat food than what's on offer in their own bowls – fat tends to make food more appetizing, even when you don't really need it.

Could the right food help wildlife?

A study carried out at the University of Exeter and published in 2021 found that a sample of pet cats who were fed a diet especially high in meat (and offered a daily play session with their owners) were less inclined to hunt wildlife outside the home.

OPPOSITE: Not too fat and not too thin; if you're not sure, your vet can confirm if your pet errs on either side.

CHOOSING THE RIGHT FOOD

So what's the best food to buy? There are dozens of commercial options, but the main choices are between dry, semi-moist and wet food. Which one suits your cat best will be down to both quality and whether or not they prefer to eat up or graze.

WHAT'S THE PAYOFF?

Learn to read the labels on commercial cat food and you can be certain you're choosing the best available diet you can afford.

What's the difference?

Dry food comes in small pellets or, more appealingly, 'biscuits'. It may suit cats who tend to graze rather than eating in one go. Its disadvantage is that it contains more cereals (padding, as they don't have nutritional benefits for cats), and dry-fed cats will need more water, so it may be less suitable for a fussy drinker. There's also some evidence that cats who graze on their meals have a greater tendency to become overweight than cats who eat their food in one go. Semi-moist food generally has a similar make-up to dry, only with a slightly higher water content. Wet food is exactly as it sounds: cooked food, often with a higher meat content and not much (if any) cereal, it comes in a wide variety of textures – advertised as 'in jelly' or 'in gravy', as 'chunks' or 'shreds' or 'paté'. It has a much stronger smell than either of the other options and the majority of cats, given the choice, prefer it.

Look at the label

Whatever type of food you buy, the illustration on the pack will show an attractive array of ingredients or an appetizing-looking bowl of carefully arranged meat or fish with vegetables. The food will be given a wholesome name, like 'Farmer's Choice', and various claims such as 'all-natural' or 'helps maintain gut health' may be used alongside it. However good it all looks, the information you want isn't to be found on the front of the package at all. Turn it over and check the label on the back instead.

The ingredients in pet food must be listed by quantity – the more of an ingredient there is, the higher it comes on the list. With cat food, you're looking for a named meat or fish – chicken, for example, or salmon, to appear at the top, and a low number of ingredients overall (if there are a lot of items on the list that you don't recognize as food, you're probably not looking at the best quality). Avoid foods which list 'derivatives' as ingredients. A label that says, for example, 'Meat and animal derivatives 90%, minimum 40% chicken' means that only 40 per cent of the meat is

OPPOSITE: A diet high in accessible protein – 'proper' meat or fish – is essential for good cat health.

guaranteed to be chicken, with a balance of unknown meat. This isn't good for those cats who have allergies, as you can't pinpoint specific ingredients, and in any case, it isn't a marker for a high-quality food. The meat that goes into pet food is rarely of the best quality anyway – despite the pictures of tasty fillets and roasted chickens that appear on the packaging, the pet-food industry uses the meat that is left over after that which is going to be used for human consumption has been removed. Despite this, when foods are sold as 'complete' cat foods, that's true: they will meet all your cat's nutritional needs, which would be hard to do if you were to put a diet together yourself, from scratch.

Go for the label with the shortest list of ingredients, with meat at the top, which doesn't also have a long list of 'unknowns' included. Commercial food makes any necessary additions of enzymes and vitamins to all recipes, so every flavour of cat food labelled as 'complete' should contain everything your cat needs – once you've checked the label, whichever flavours your cat prefers should give them what they need nutritionally.

Raw and home-cooked

Of course, there's another option: you can feed your cat raw food. This tends to divide owners. Some worry that uncooked food is more likely to contain bacteria that will make your cat ill, while others maintain that it's the most natural way to feed an animal which, in the wild, would be living on mice, voles and the occasional bird or bat. If you'd like to try it but you're dubious, check in with your vet first, then look for one of the higher-end suppliers who are very clear about what their food contains (usually meat with a little ground bone and sometimes a small quantity of vegetables). It tends to arrive in trays or plastic rolls, ready for the freezer if you're buying in any quantity, which can then simply be defrosted in the amounts you need. Making your cat raw meals from scratch calls for rather more research (and a lot of chopping or mincing) so is probably only for the most dedicated. Try the raw diet out on your cat before committing – while some cats love it, others are firm in their preference for cooked meals.

OPPOSITE: **If your cat tends to be capricious about what they will or won't eat, try to establish several different foods they generally like, so that you can offer them on rota.**

Fish flavours

Cats don't fish in the wild, and fish wouldn't form part of a feral cat's diet, so why is fish the main ingredient of so many cat foods? Partly because, like other meats, fish still provides animal protein containing many of the elements that your cat needs, and partly because cats almost universally seem to find most fish very appetizing.

If you want to feed fresh fish as part of a home-cooked meal, it should be cooked (raw fish contains an enzyme which destroys thiamine, a substance that is necessary for cats' health), and picked through carefully to remove fine bones – which pose the same choking hazard to cats as they do to us.

SNACKS & TREATS

All cats enjoy treats but don't turn yours into a nag by becoming an automatic dispenser; keep treats as just that – a small, occasional indulgence. And check the label first, to make sure the ingredients are recognizable and there aren't too many unknowns.

Easy snacks

Not all treats need to come out of a packet, however, and there isn't much point in being extremely scrupulous about your cat's day-to-day meals but then throwing caution to the wind when it comes to extras. The 'don't feed from the table' is a rule that holds just as strongly for cats as it does for dogs: if you don't want a chorus of entitled mewing when the roast chicken is laid down, then don't encourage your cat to think that it's theirs. Instead, plan ahead and put some suitable offerings aside when you're cooking your own meals: tiny scraps of cooked chicken or fish, unseasoned, are likely to go down well, and can be kept in the fridge for a day or two. Don't dismiss vegetables, either – plenty of cats enjoy vegetable trimmings, such as carrot ends, a single French bean or a cabbage leaf. They'll use them as a sort of combination toy-and-snack, pushing them around and chasing them, while nibbling them too.

Tuna madness

Tuna invariably tops the list when it comes to every cat's favourite fish. It can compromise a cat's absorption of vitamin E, however, so only feed your cat tuna when it's an ingredient in balanced commercial cat food or in specially prepared homemade treats (see page 87).

OPPOSITE: Keep treats small but high-value; dry kibble doesn't usually act as much of a motivator.

Hot-weather refreshers

In very hot weather your cat will probably enjoy a feline ice lolly. You can make them by freezing salt-free meat broth, including a few small pieces of meat, into ice trays. Keep them in the freezer, and give your pet one or two cubes to help cool them down on boiling hot days.

Portion control

Treats, even healthy ones, should make up no more than 10 per cent of your cat's daily intake, so make the ones you offer count. One advantage of the homemade variety is that you can easily break them up (an appropriate-sized treat is smaller than you might imagine – pea-sized is good), so you can keep intake low while maintaining a generous reputation with your cat.

WHAT'S THE PAYOFF?

Learn to read the labels on commercial cat food and you can be certain you're choosing the best available diet you can afford.

MAKE YOUR OWN CAT TREATS

If you want to be comfortable about what's in the treats you feed your cat, you can make your own. And while cooking a complete balanced diet for a cat may be too much for most owners, making a couple of types of treat is both quick and straightforward.

Liver and parsley bites

Organ meats are good for cats, and some parsley has been added here as a breath sweetener (nice for you, and your cat won't mind). Rice flour is more digestible for cats than most wheat flours. The mixture makes quite a lot of rich treats, so after it's been cooked and cut into pieces, put any that won't be eaten within a day or two into small bags, freeze them and defrost as needed.

INGREDIENTS

- 250g (9oz) chicken livers
- 1 egg
- 2 tbsp parsley, finely chopped
- 120g (4oz) rice flour

Preheat the oven to 180°C/160°C/350°F/ gas mark 4. Grease a small roasting tin (around 30 x 20cm/12 x 8in).

Use a blender or a stick blender to mix the livers and the egg together thoroughly, then transfer to a mixing bowl.

Stir in the parsley, then sift in the flour and mix thoroughly.

Scrape the mixture into the tin and smooth it into a thin, even layer.

Bake for around 20 minutes, checking after 15 minutes that the treats aren't overcooking.

Take out of the oven, leave in the tin until completely cold, then turn the mixture out and cut into small cubes, around 1-cm (½-in) square.

Tuna meringue treats

The 'meringue' in the title refers to the fact that these treats are made using beaten egg white. They don't contain any carbohydrate, and they're light and palatable. Keep them in the fridge and use them within about ten days – although they may not last that long.

INGREDIENTS

- 1 egg
- 1 x 120g (4oz) tin tuna in spring water (avoid tuna in brine or oil)

Preheat the oven to 180°C/160°C fan/350°F/ gas mark 4. Line a large baking tray with baking parchment.

Separate the egg white from the yolk.

Use a stick blender to mix the tuna with some of the egg yolk, adding the latter bit by bit. Stop when you have a smoothish, thickish paste (you may not need to use all of the yolk).

In a separate clean bowl, whisk the egg white until it forms stiff peaks.

Using a metal spoon, fold one spoonful of the egg white into the tuna/egg yolk mixture to loosen it, then carefully fold in the rest.

Using a teaspoon, spoon coin-sized quantities of the mixture onto the lined baking tray and bake for 20 minutes, checking halfway through the cooking time.

Leave to cool before storing in a lidded container in the fridge.

FOOD PUZZLES

Nothing can ever quite replace a chase-and-tackle game for most cats, but a good food puzzle, whether bought or homemade, can come close, and at times when you're not around to play, it will offer a welcome distraction in an otherwise dull day.

How smart is your cat?

Every pet shop has a wide range of food puzzles – from simple ball dispensers, which can be rolled around with a paw to make the treats drop out, to complex mazes featuring compartments with different lids and knobs which must be pushed or pulled to open. They can be filled with a portion of your cat's regular food (there's no reason why your pet can't do a little work for it), with dry treats or with small dabs of wet food, and it's entertaining to watch a clever cat figure them out – or a slightly less smart cat try. Quite how keen your cat is to tackle one of these puzzles will come down to how food-motivated or hungry they are, but if you fill one with something you know your cat loves, the incentive should be enough for them to give it a try.

Start with the simpler options and see how your pet gets on – some will graduate to the more challenging puzzles, others won't. In the meantime, you can also use various pieces of packaging to create your own homemade puzzle options.

WHAT'S THE PAYOFF?

There's some evidence that cats who love a puzzle like to hone their skills, so if your first offering is a success, you may find you've tapped into a long-term interest.

HOMEMADE FOOD PUZZLES

You can hide a treat or two in an unwanted cardboard box, or among scrunched up paper packaging (see pages 38–9), and most food-motivated cats will hunt them out. There are several other instant food puzzles that you can make for your cat that will take (very) slightly more effort on your part, too – although they're usually quick to solve, they should still offer a few minutes' worth of entertainment.

• Take a cardboard roll from either toilet paper or kitchen roll, tuck in one end with your thumbs, then drop in two or three small cat treats and tuck the other end in so that the tube is sealed. Use sharp scissors to cut a hole in the side of the roll just big enough for a treat to drop through, then shake it so that the rattle attracts your cat's attention and give it to them to figure out.

• Wrap six small treats in crumpled up newspaper, then take a cardboard egg box, put one treat in each hollow of the box, close the lid and pass it to your cat.

• Take a plastic mug with a handle and put a smear of meat or fish paste (the kind sold for cats, not humans) inside it, about halfway down. Lay it on its side on a piece of newspaper or a feeding mat, and let your cat work out how to get the contents out. The handle will stop it rolling around too much while your pet solves the problem.

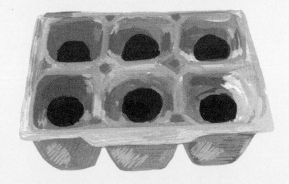

If you're making a food puzzle, be as creative as you like; it should keep your cat intrigued while they work it out.

WHAT CATS DON'T EAT

Perhaps this should be 'shouldn't eat' rather than 'don't eat'; the problem arises because, given the chance, cats will still eat a number of toxic things. Some you may already know about, but others aren't so widely publicized.

Leave well alone

We all know that curiosity killed the cat; perhaps it caused him to consume something he should have left alone. Don't let your pet eat:

• Houseplants
These got a mention in the third chapter. Most cats enjoy greenery in their everyday surroundings, but every year a number of pet cats are poisoned by toxic plants that they decided to nibble on. By all means enjoy your houseplants, but ensure they aren't poisonous to pets before you bring them home (there are plenty of comprehensive pet-safe plant checklists to be found online).

• Chocolate
Almost everyone knows about dogs and chocolate, but not so many know that chocolate is toxic to cats, too – just like dogs, they are unable to digest the theobromine it contains. The higher the percentage of cocoa solids, the more dangerous the chocolate.

• Dairy products

Despite the time-honoured image of a cat lapping at a saucer of milk, dairy products – including milk, cream and yoghurt – all contain lactase, which cats can't digest. Most can lick out an empty yoghurt carton without coming to harm, but larger quantities aren't a good idea. Cheese, in which the lactase has mostly been 'cooked' away in the manufacturing process, can be given as an occasional treat, but only in tiny amounts.

Dog food isn't for cats

Don't feed your cat commercial dog food, even for the occasional meal; although the tins or trays of wet food may look (and smell) very similar, nutritionally they're quite different, and dog food just doesn't do an adequate job for a cat.

• Grapes and raisins

No one knows why these can be toxic to cats – sometimes they can be eaten without ill-effects, sometimes just one or two grapes or a few raisins can cause kidney failure. Don't play Russian roulette with your pet's health by leaving them around; keep them safely in the fridge or the cupboard.

• Onions and garlic

Onions can cause anaemia in cats, as can garlic, and although they're unlikely to form a regular part of your cat's diet, their toxicity is a good reason not to feed your cat leftovers of human foods such as casseroles or stews, in which they're often ingredients.

• Xylitol

This natural sweetener is highly toxic to cats; because many brands of peanut butter contain it, it's one reason not to feed peanut butter as a cat treat. Go for small shreds of chicken instead.

FAT CAT TO FIT CAT

Do you know what your cat weighs? The number of overweight cats is unfortunately on the rise – some estimates put it at one in three – but it's a problem that can be fairly easily solved if you take decisive charge of it.

The ideal weight

General guides tell you that the 'average' cat weighs around 4.5kg (10lb), but a small, slender Tonkinese might weigh in at less and a comparatively hefty Norwegian Forest cat more, and both might still be a healthy weight for their size and build. Looking at them (and, if they're fluffy, feeling them) will tell you what you need to know.

Look at your cat sideways on: they should have a visible 'waist' – a noticeable rise behind the ribs. If you stroke them firmly along their sides, you should also be able to feel their ribs easily. If your cat has both a waist and defined ribs, they're probably at a reasonable weight. If they are carrying more padding, you can take action to get them back in shape.

From kitten to veteran

Because cats have quite complex food needs, these often change across their lifetime. Food sold specifically for kittens – usually categorized as cats under a year old – is more calorie-dense; food for older cats is often lower in calories. But cats can also develop a range of food-related conditions and allergies, and they aren't usually noisy about their problems. If your cat seems to be losing weight when they don't need to, or drinking more or less than usual, or if there's any other change in what they usually eat or drink that lasts more than two or three days, get them checked.

FOUR WAYS TO HELP

Cats should lose weight slowly – rapid weight loss can lead to liver problems – so don't look for fast results, and check in with your vet before cutting their food. Once you know how much, and what, they should be eating, try the following tips.

1. Increase activity. Especially if your pet is an indoor cat, take part yourself by spending three or four ten-minute sessions every day playing with them – fishing rods and lure poles, balls and wrestling toys will all help to raise activity levels.

2. If you've been in the habit of leaving food down for them to eat whenever they like, start feeding them two meals a day, removing the food bowl after twenty minutes. 'On demand' feeders have a greater tendency to be overweight. It may feel mean at first, but your cat will soon get used to the new schedule. Make sure they always have access to clean water.

3. Consider feeding some of their food in a food puzzle. If they eat dried food, you could also try scattering a handful of their biscuits outside, so that they have to 'hunt' for them.

4. Don't guess quantities; weigh it out. 'Half a pouch' of food can easily turn into three-quarters if you're not concentrating.

Although older cats can be prone to losing weight, statistically far more cats are over- rather than underweight.

WHAT'S THE PAYOFF?

A cat who is a healthy weight will lead a happier, and often a longer, life. Express your affection with games rather than extra food, and your pet's increased energy levels will reflect the difference.

REST & RELAXATION

Cats used to be known as easy pets – mostly when compared to dogs. They don't ask for walks, they often seem content with their own company and however pleased they are to see 'their' humans, most of them still carry an air of self-sufficiency. Now that we're starting to understand more about their needs and the different signals they send, however, it's becoming harder to argue that they're best left to their own devices.

This chapter looks at ways to ensure that your shared space feels safe and comfortable to your cat – whether they're meeting their epic sleeping needs, quietly hanging out or opting to spend one-on-one time with you.

A HOME THAT SMELLS RIGHT

Cats spend a lot of time making sure their surroundings smell familiar. Whenever they rub their cheeks on a surface or slink along a wall making contact with it all the way, they're laying down their scent.

WHAT'S THE PAYOFF?

Even though you can't smell them, the scents your cat leaves around the house are markers of comfort. Return the favour by keeping your shared environment clear of too many harsh, manufactured smells, while leaving some of your cat's own signals in place.

To your cat, surroundings that are generously self-scented help their home to feel safe and familiar.

The scent glands on different parts of a cat do different jobs. Those between their paw pads are used when they're scratching and are thought to be connected to territory-marking and finding a mate, as are those around the back end of a cat, on the flanks and around the tail. The action you're most familiar with in your own cat, the head rubbing – or bunting – that's performed dozens of times a day, uses the scent glands on their cheeks and foreheads, and around their mouths, to deposit friendly smells. It's believed that these are the 'comfortable territory' scents with which they anoint people and places with whom they are at ease. A head rub from your cat is a compliment – one which can be repaid with a gentle ear rub.

Clean – but not too clean

You probably like your environment to be clean, and most people use products beyond soap and elbow grease to keep it that way. After a phenomenal rise in heavily scented specialist cleaners for everything from glass to wood to upholstery, the pendulum seems to be swinging back to more environmentally friendly options. Your cat is likely to prefer them, too. Strong smells can drown out their scent trails; you can help by watching for some of their favourite bunting spots – the sides of doorways, or that place on the bannisters where they always pause to head-rub – and leaving them uncleaned. Avoid plug-in diffusers (which belch out smells at cat's-nose level) and powerfully scented incense or candles. Not very much research has been done on cats' responses to these, but it's a safe bet that they disrupt a cat's refined scenting sense, and that your pet would prefer soap-washed and line-dried fabrics and open windows to allow in outdoor scents.

Helpful scents

The exception to the broad no-diffusers rule are those produced with the aim of lowering stress levels in pet cats. Owners use them for all kinds of reasons – in anticipation of their pet's fear of fireworks around big holidays; as an attempted aid to stop cats spraying or toileting in the house, or as an all-round calmer. The scents they diffuse mimic a cat's natural facial markers. Do they work? It's a qualified yes, but for serious problems like spraying, take a vet's advice before you try them, and if you're using them for a specific event, such as fireworks, plug them in a day or two beforehand to give your cat a chance to adjust – and be calmed.

THE POWER OF ROUTINE

Cats need enrichment and occasional surprises in their lives, but research has shown that they do better if these come against the background of a solid routine. Getting the balance right is tricky and may vary, cat to cat.

Keep things predictable

If cats have a regular routine, and know when to expect food and play, it generally suits them better than a more random timetable. This idea took root following the result of one well-known study, conducted over a year and a half, and published by the American Veterinary Medical Association in 2011, which took a sample of thirty-two cats and gave them a regular daily routine – they could reliably expect that the same person would be caring for them, and predict when they would be fed, played with, when their litter trays would be cleaned, and so on. Twelve were in good health; the other twenty suffered from a chronic condition that led to them needing to pee frequently, along with various other symptoms, and for which there was no treatment.

With a carefully arranged daily routine in which everything ran like clockwork, the researchers were surprised to find that not only did the well cats thrive, but the sick ones steadily improved until many of the symptoms of their condition no longer manifested. Knowing exactly what to expect and when seemed to result in a huge reduction in all the cats' stress levels – which, in turn, raised the question of whether all cats experience a high level of stress when leading what seem to us to be quite normal day-to-day lives. When the reliable regime was replaced by one which was deliberately disrupted – for example, the schedule of mealtimes was thrown out by an hour or two (although they still received regular meals), or they were looked after by someone they weren't used to – not only did the sick cats start displaying all their old symptoms, but the 'well' cats also began to show signs of stress, vomiting, failing to use their litter boxes, and so on.

What's the lesson?

Cats have hard-to-read faces (to us, anyway), and we're only just learning about a lot of what makes them tick, but the takeaway from this study seemed to be that cats may be a lot more anxious than we think, and the answer to reducing their stress levels – with commensurate improvements in their all-round physical health – is to give them the reassurance of a regular routine. Of course, that doesn't mean their lives should be boring, but it seems that a solid supporting framework suits them best.

WHAT'S THE PAYOFF?

A set routine doesn't mean that your cat won't enjoy novelty and (good) surprises, but giving them a framework so they know when they can expect meals, your undivided attention and undisturbed nap times seems to suit pet cats best.

Even a cat who's given to sudden extravagant bursts of activity probably has a fairly regular underlying routine. Research has shown that cats thrive when they – mostly – know what to expect.

WHEN TO PET
(AND WHEN TO STOP)

Some cats love to be petted, are content to sit on a human lap and will enjoy – or at least endure – any amount of fuss. Others seem happy to be around humans but don't enjoy being touched, and still others are shy of human contact altogether.

Whether or not a cat enjoys fuss from a human is a mix of nature and nurture: a cat from shy parents who wasn't extensively socialized in early kittenhood probably won't ever be as relaxed as one from sociable parents who was heavily socialized. This doesn't mean that you have to forego contact altogether, although the former example may never become a fully fledged lapcat.

Making friends

Don't pick up an unwilling cat, don't try to make them stay anywhere they don't want to and don't let anyone else do that either, or you'll end up forcing the cat to strike out. Ouch. Instead, look at the places in which they do enjoy relaxing. Do they have a favourite cushion or rug? Can you move it nearer to you and add something they like – a catnip mouse, perhaps? A food puzzle toy? The more inviting you make the area around you, the more likely they are to sit nearby.

Lashing out, and how to stop it

It's happened to everyone: your cat seemed to be enjoying contact and you'd moved from a gentle scritch around the head to stroking their chest, when they suddenly swung at your hand with an irritable paw, claws very much unsheathed, or, worse, bit you, wriggled and ran off. What did you do wrong, and can you stop it from happening again?

OPPOSITE: You know that you've reached peak pet security when your cat trusts you enough to fall asleep on your lap.

Petting a cat is never entirely risk-free, but you can reduce the chances.

1. Look out for triggers: a cat may switch their tail, turn to look at you or ripple their muscles visibly. None of these is a good sign – stop petting, withdraw your hand, then leave your cat to decide what to do.

2. Watch where you touch a cat. Many will enjoy their cheeks or ears being rubbed, but most are less keen on being stroked along their sides, and very few like being handled on their paws, belly or tail.

3. Keep any petting session short, around five minutes, then stop completely, even if your cat solicits more. They may then opt to stay with you, enjoying the proximity.

Why?

No one knows exactly why cats suddenly turn against something that they've seem to be enjoying, but there are a couple of theories. One is that repeated stroking builds up static, which the cat experiences as small, unpleasant shocks; the other is that cats become overstimulated, making a pleasant sensation suddenly irritating. Learn to spot the danger signs.

WHAT'S THE PAYOFF?

Even a naturally standoffish cat can learn to enjoy being near you if there are evident benefits – work with what your pet *does* like, rather than pushing something they don't.

COMFORTABLE GROOMING

Your cat probably spends a couple of hours every day grooming themselves. Do you need to step in and groom them too? Yes, at least occasionally – or more often if your pet is elderly, long-haired, or enjoys nocturnal excursions through deep undergrowth.

Get the right kit

Depending on the kind of coat your cat has, you may find that you're best served by a silicone or rubber grooming glove (usually made from mesh or loose weave, with a palmful of soft 'bristles'), or a small silicone brush with a strap that you can slide over your hand. This may even be enough for a short-haired cat with no tendency to mat – silicone in particular is good at picking up loose cat hair, so that you don't scatter it around as you groom. For longer-haired or fluffier cats you're likely to need a fine-toothed brush and/or comb, plus a pair of blunt scissors (and possibly some talcum powder which makes it easier to get through the edges of the clump) to take out potential mats, but a grooming glove is usually a good start to a session, as most cats enjoy it.

Dealing with mats

Mats are the felted clumps of hair that can build up without regular grooming. Serious mats should be dealt with by the vet (it's easy to nick the skin if you try to cut them out); slightly matted hair can be very gently combed out from the edges before the centre is carefully cut out.

WHAT'S THE PAYOFF?

Little and often will ensure that grooming is at least a bearable experience for both of you – some cats come to actively enjoy it – and helps to avoid matting and expensive visits to the professionals.

The soft spines of a grooming glove are a good way to introduce a wary cat to very gentle grooming.

Keeping it painless

The best way to make grooming stress-free is to start (very) slow and then stay absolutely regular with it. If your cat has been groomed since they were a kitten, they'll probably be accepting of the routine, especially if you begin when they're already relaxed and use bribery over the course of the session. If you didn't own your cat as a kitten, you may find that the grooming glove is your friend – cats seem to find the gentle brushing sensation quite pleasant, and if you introduce it as a very brief feature when you're making a regular fuss of your cat, then gradually raise the time you spend grooming and reduce the amount of non-grooming fuss, they may not even notice that something different is going on. Pick a time when your cat is relaxed but not actually asleep, and do a minute or two daily, concentrating on the least sensitive parts of the body (usually around the head and shoulders), building up very gradually to longer sessions, and more sensitive areas, as your cat gets used to it.

CAN YOUR CAT LEARN?

Cats are very astute in the lessons they take away from real-life situations – but the question is, can your cat learn from you? The answer, fairly thoroughly researched over the last few years, is yes: if you have the patience to teach, your cat has the ability to learn.

Training to make your cat happy

Cats have long had a reputation for being untrainable ('like herding cats' is a traditional saying for a reason), but the likely truth is that nobody had tried to train them until comparatively recently, when books by some very dedicated researchers established that cats certainly can be trained, or rather encouraged and conditioned, into a whole range of behaviours – using methods not very different from those used when training dogs.

The question might be, why would you want to train your cat? You might like to use some training as a way to extend the bond you already have, to replace a behaviour you don't like (it's possible to train a cat to get in and out of their carrier without drama, for example, which can greatly reduce the stress – for them and for you – of visits to the vet), to create a behaviour you want, or, experimentally, simply for fun. From your cat's point of view, with appropriate motivation and really high-quality rewards, structured learning becomes just another positive activity. And with the right approach, most cats learn to enjoy training with 'their' humans.

OPPOSITE: Keeping a travel crate around as part of your cat's everyday furniture will condition them to be comfortable around it.

Starting out

Whole books have been written on the subject of training (some using clicker training, some not – and of course training with clickers is a whole subject in itself); a few pages here can only give the broadest picture, but if you'd like to try to teach your cat, here are some – broad and brief – guidelines. If they spark an interest in the pair of you, hunt out a good book – there are some suggestions on page 128 – set up a regular teaching slot, and see how you get on.

In the beginning, set yourself up for success by choosing a time when your cat is in a receptive mood – this means neither right before nor right after a meal (when they'll be too hungry or too full), not while they're napping, and not when their attention is already strongly engaged by something else. Pick a quiet spot without any obvious distractions (not by the window where the birdfeeder hangs) and arm yourself with something really good that your cat doesn't get all the time – tuna treats perhaps, or a new toy that you're pretty sure they'll love.

WHAT'S THE PAYOFF?

Training with your cat, in a way that ensures they're an enthusiastic participant, can help to build the bond between you and prove absorbing for you both. If you take it a bit further, it can also be a really valuable tool in helping to desensitize your cat to things that stress them.

Small goals

Keep your expectations small and set both you and your cat up for the win. You might begin, for example, by aiming to get your cat to come when called, or to 'ask' for a treat with a high five. Your cat can already come when called, as you know if you've ever rustled a treat packet – and, broken down, the training is doing exactly the same thing, except you'll be replacing the rustle with a sound you've chosen – it might be a clicker, if you have one, or simply a specific noise, such as a chirrup or a tongue click. Whatever you choose, stick to it. After that, it's unbelievably simple:

• **Keep the treats at hand**, break them into minute pieces, but be generous with the number to start with.
• **Stand three steps away** from your cat (no more, no less).
• **Make your chosen noise**. When they look up, show them a treat, and if they move towards you, give it to them. Time it tightly; give the treat as quickly as possible after the approach, as you want to make the connection between their action and the reward in their mind.
• **Take a step further away**, make the noise again (and have a treat ready). If your cat comes towards you, give them the treat. If they don't, step forward again, and repeat the first step.
• **Carry on in tiny increments**. Each one may take lots of repetitions, but don't try to run (or rather get your cat to run) before you can walk. Across a week or two, being consistent with the noise you make and the treats you offer, and very, very gradually increasing the distance your cat has to travel to get the reward, you should succeed in getting your cat to come, even from some way away, to the signal you make. This may not even sound like training to you, but you've successfully reinforced a behaviour you wanted from your cat, so it is.

Don't let any training session go over a maximum of ten minutes (five is fine). You'll maintain your cat's concentration much better if you keep things short.

TRY A HIGH FIVE

If you want to try a 'trick', then the high five is probably the easiest. You can teach this one with treats or with a toy – it's a good use of the long-fingered gloves that appeared in the second chapter.

• Start when your cat is already paying you attention, but on the floor, rather than on a chair or your lap.

• Put on a long-fingered glove, or have a large feather or a small toy your cat likes to hand.

• Let's say you're using the long-fingered glove. Hold it just over your cat's head and wave one finger slightly. If you choose a feather or a toy, just hold it between your thumb and forefinger and do the same thing. Watch out for your fingers.

• Your cat will look up and likely 'dab' at the finger. At the exact instant they do it, make a click of your tongue (or use a clicker, if you've got enough hands and you're used to clickers!) and 'reward' with an extra wave of the finger.

• If they don't dab at first, wait till they do, 'resting' the glove (or the hand holding the feather) between tries – you don't want this to turn into a general pouncing game.

• Gradually narrow down the 'clicks' you make to 'reward' only those dabs that resemble a high-five. Increasingly, less accurate dabs will result in interaction with the glove, feather or toy, stopping. Eventually – it can take a lot of tries – your cat will narrow down the paw gesture that gets the click – and more play – and they'll have mastered the high-five.

If you find that your cat is a quick learner, experiment with different sorts of tricks to keep them entertained and build up their repertoire.

LIFE STAGES

The previous chapters each took an aspect of a cat's life, from eating to playing, resting to fitness, and looked at ways you could best understand your pet and make their life happier in each category. This last section is different: it's an overview of a few specific issues or times in a cat's life. Not all of it will apply to every reader: you may have neither a kitten nor an elderly cat right now. But when you do – and, as a cat custodian, the time will come – there are some tips here that you'll remember, whether they're about socializing kittens, making an elderly cat comfortable, or settling in a new cat alongside a well-established one.

A CAT'S LIFE

The oldest cat on record – Creme Puff, of Austin, Texas – made it past her thirty-eighth birthday. While she was exceptional, the life expectancy of pet cats has risen over the last four decades, and a cat that lives into its 20s is no longer especially unusual, while between 12 and 17 has become the norm.

Sustained care

Despite their increased longevity, pet cats pay far fewer visits to the vet over their lifetime than pet dogs, although it's never really been established why there's a difference. It may be because of cats' longstanding – and not entirely justified – reputation as low-maintenance pets (largely because they aren't given daily walks), or their semi-domesticated status, or because cats, even more than dogs, tend to hide away when they're ill and make themselves less available for observation. There's even an argument that it's the result of cats being harder to take to the vet than dogs: you can't just snap the lead onto a reluctant animal and go; instead, there's the whole finding-and-coaxing-into-the-carrier routine to get through.

So how often does a cat need a vet visit? Even if they're not ill, a cat still needs vaccinations, and annual or bi-annual check-ups (depending on their age and general state of health) – remind yourself that preventative care tends to save money in the long run, as well as sparing your cat pain, even if these are the appointments that don't feel quite so essential at the time. When it comes to home care, the two most important things you can do to keep your cat in good health is to take care of their teeth (see page 70–71) and feed them the best diet you can afford.

OPPOSITE: **Your cat's life stages can seem to pass extraordinarily fast: from leaf-chasing kitten to calmer veteran without you consciously noticing.**

Fear-free vets

Earlier chapters talked about getting your pet used to their carrier to make travel easier for them. Look at what happens when they arrive at the vet's surgery, too. Increasingly vets are acknowledging that visits can be traumatic for pets and taking steps to make them less so. When you register with a vet, ask plenty of questions. Two phrases to look out for are 'fear-free' and 'low-stress handling', referring to the ways in which vets themselves can reduce the fear of a visit, both in the way they handle a cat, and looking at the set-up within the consulting room – from providing more comfortable surfaces to offering distraction techniques.

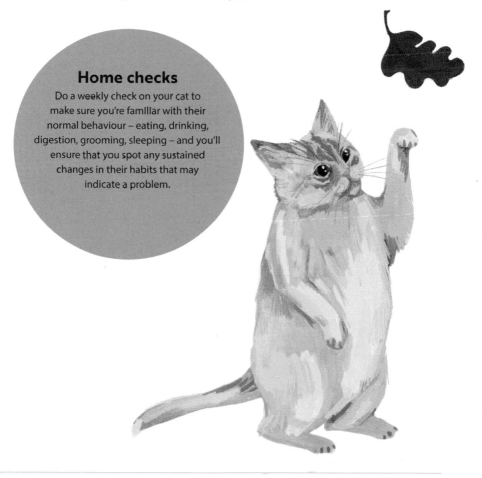

Home checks

Do a weekly check on your cat to make sure you're familiar with their normal behaviour – eating, drinking, digestion, grooming, sleeping – and you'll ensure that you spot any sustained changes in their habits that may indicate a problem.

KITTEN IN THE HOUSE

Arguably, you need to do more proofing for a kitten than a puppy – after all, even the most athletic pup is unlikely to climb halfway up the curtains. Write a checklist and make sure you've ticked everything off before your kitten's paws are through the door.

No space too small

The most surprising thing about kittens is just how small a space they can fit into. Add insatiable curiosity and excellent climbing skills to this, and you have a recipe for... all kinds of accidents. It's usually a good idea to confine your kitten to a single room when they first arrive, with plenty of visits of course, until they've found their feet. It also gives you some time to identify problem areas elsewhere in the house, and to cat-proof those (keep dishwasher and washing/drying machines closed, and the loo seat down). When you've decided on which room, check it. Look up: are there high shelves? Bookcases? Anything a kitten could brush by and break? Take ornaments down and shut them in a cupboard for the time being. Then look around at kitten-eye level. Sockets should be off, and wires and leads should be unplugged, rolled up, and held by a rubber band so they don't offer tempting ends for chewing and chasing; do the same with blind cords. Remove plants unless you're absolutely certain they're non-toxic for cats (even if they are, you don't want your kitten deciding that they look like small litter trays, so plants may be best off-limits altogether for now).

Next, check for hiding places. Every kitten owner has had the panicky experience of a locked-room mystery: no route of escape, and yet no kitten. Tiny, tiny spaces are accessible – look for gaps behind radiators, small spaces under bookshelves, and so on, and block any tricky ones off. Larger

OPPOSITE: Offering a new kitten some obvious places to 'hide' makes for an enjoyable game for both of you.

hiding spaces – under the bed, for example – are fine; it's natural for a kitten to want to hide, but there should be no risk of them getting stuck.

After a few days, leave the door open so that your kitten can start to explore the (by now kitten-proofed) house. Engage in very regular play and treat sessions so that the kitten gets used to the idea that you'll provide fun to order, and wants to spend most of their time with you nearby.

Kitten-sized

Scale down your kitten's feeding and water bowls and litter tray. The litter tray should still be roomy, but not outsized. Feeding and water bowls should be big enough for a kitten meal, but not so big that a kitten is tempted to paddle in them. Beds don't matter so much if there are plenty of rugs and blankets to snuggle into – like adult cats, kittens often opt to sleep in a warm corner rather than a bed, in any case.

WHAT'S THE PAYOFF?

If everything is well prepared before your kitten shows up, you'll spend more time enjoying their company and much less time frantically rushing to move things out of reach.

STARTING YOUNG
KITTEN SOCIALIZATION

Kittens are so appealing in their non-stop, cartoon-like activity that it's easy to forget they're immersed in rapid learning every day. Their lived experiences will affect their behaviour for the long term, so it's a good idea to shape these in a positive way.

WHAT'S THE PAYOFF?

A well-socialized kitten should be able to cope with a whole range of different people and experiences as they mature; those early weeks are crucial in helping them to take a confident and calm approach to the wider world.

The stages of kittenhood

Although kittens often leave their mothers and go to new owners once they're fully weaned at around eight weeks old, most breeders of pedigree cats only send them off to their homes at twelve or thirteen weeks – and that's because young kittens are still taking lessons from both their mother and their siblings; they're learning how to be cats, which will be especially important later on if they're to live comfortably with other cats. While their mother demonstrates key skills – how to hunt, for example, and how to bury their waste in a different place from where they eat and play – and their fellow kittens help to develop their play skills and draw boundaries if play gets too sharp or bitey, which may save you the trouble of having to do it later on, the ideal socialization for a kitten also includes plenty of encounters, including handling, with different people. It's also good for them to meet other (friendly) animals while they're still very young; the more familiar they are, the better they'll be able to negotiate relationships with dogs, and cats outside their immediate family, when they're adults.

The right sort of touch

An adult cat's relationship with people depends to a large extent on how much they were handled and played with as a kitten. Consistent, gentle handling every day, from a variety of people, including children, is probably the most valuable experience you can offer. Individual personality will always be a big factor: some kittens are naturally more placid and accepting than others. But rescuers have found that even feral kittens who haven't had their start in a home can be tamed over a few weeks with regular handling.

How to handle a kitten

At four or five weeks, a kitten will usually settle into a gentle, firm hold quickly and snuggle down. As kittens get older, they're less likely to relax so speedily and it may be easier to cuddle them after you've played for a while. Keep the habit of regular play-and-handling sessions as your kitten matures. Aim for several ten-minute sessions every day (if young children are involved, ensure they're gentle, so the kitten won't be frightened) and your cat will have every chance of being comfortable around people as an adult.

OPPOSITE: Make sure you handle and play with a new kitten regularly but not incessantly – don't forget that new experiences are tiring for them and take time to absorb.

MORE THAN ONE

In the main, this book has looked at cats kept as single pets. However, although wild cats led solitary lives in the past, coming together only to sort out territorial disputes or to mate, today's pets can be much more social, and some actively need company.

Sometimes getting two cats is as easy as adopting two kittens from the same litter – siblings tend to get along well, as they've been with each other, sharing the same experiences (and, crucially for cats, the same smells) from the start. Or if you go to a rescue centre for an adult cat, they may occasionally suggest that two cats that get along well be adopted together. If that's not your situation, though, and you have a solo cat but feel that they'd like a friend, it may take careful introductions and often more time than you'd imagined – several weeks, or even a couple of months – to make your cats reasonably comfortable with each other. Provided you're patient and prepared to take it at both cats' respective paces, you should end up with a successful result.

Doubling up

Whether your cat will easily accept a newcomer or not, you'll certainly need to double up on the facilities. Don't assume that things can be shared – it may happen over time, but in the beginning both cats will feel safer using different feeding and water bowls and litter trays, beds and even cat trees, and will usually opt to rest in different places, at least for a while. Cats may opt to block one another's access to a litter box or a water bowl as a way of staking out their own territory, so each litter box and so on also needs to be in a different location, ensuring that both cats can have access to what they need while everything is settling down. The idea of two cat friends curling up together straight away is appealing but unlikely.

WHAT'S THE PAYOFF?

If your cat is one of those that craves company, and especially if you're out of the house for prolonged periods, a carefully introduced friend will make sure they're not lonely and give them someone of their own species to play with.

Adult cats need to be introduced to one another carefully; even if they don't become best friends most, given time and space, can learn to tolerate one another.

EIGHT STEPS TO INTRODUCE A NEW CAT

1. Prepare a room in which the new cat can stay for the first few days, with a clean litter tray, water, and comfortable places to rest, along with a catnip toy. You could also leave a few treats scattered about. Stair gates will be useful while you're getting cats used to one another, so borrow a couple if possible.

2. When you bring the new cat into the house, take them straight into the room, shut the door and open the carrier (make sure your own cat doesn't shoot into the room while you're letting the new cat out).

3. For the first couple of days, keep the new cat in their own room, going in to feed them and play with them if they're willing to engage. It's completely normal for them to want to hide; if they don't want to come out from under the bed or behind a chair, leave them be – sit down quietly and read a book for half an hour. This will help them get used to your presence and encourage them to see you as 'safe'.

4. When the new cat is prepared to get close to you and be petted a little, take a clean duster and rub it very gently over them, concentrating on the areas around their ears, cheeks and chin, so the cloth takes on their smell, then take it to a room your cat uses a lot and leave it there, in an accessible spot where it's available to sniff at.

5. Repeat the duster-rub, but this time on your own cat. Take this second duster into the room where the new cat is settling in.

6. After a day or two, when the cats have had the chance to get used to each other's scent, put up a stair gate in the door of the new cat's room while you're in there; this allows your old cat to see them from a distance. Shut the door when you're not nearby, but when it's in your sightline, use the gate.

7. Get some highly desirable treats and offer them to both cats on either side of the barrier, throwing them a fair distance away from each side, so the cats don't need to get too near one another.

8. It may take a few days or a couple of weeks, but slowly you should see signs that the cats are showing non-hostile curiosity. Start leaving the door to the new cat's room open when you're nearby, without using the stair gate, and offer (separate) treats and toys if the cats are in the same vicinity. Over time, you'll relax and so will they.

Sometimes it's easy

What's described opposite is the slow route. If your existing cat is easy-going and not especially territorial, and the new cat is similarly fairly placid, you may find that the whole process can be condensed into a day or two – occasionally, a new cat will arrive in an established household with no fanfare whatsoever. You'll spot the signs of cats willing to be friendly: relaxed body language with no 'chat' (spitting, hissing or puffing themselves up), and a willingness to be near one another and to relax in the same room. When they're prepared to share a sofa or a sunny windowsill, even at a slight distance, you'll know that the settling-in process is almost complete.

Don't assume there will be difficulties: sometimes two easygoing cats will form a relationship more quickly than you expected.

WILDLIFE-PROOFING YOUR CAT

It's a discussion that every cat owner will have got into at one time or another: does your cat hunt, bringing in birds and small mammals on a regular basis, and if so, at a time when biodiversity is in sharp decline, is there anything you can do to stop it?

WHAT'S THE PAYOFF?

Distraction and play tactics may work as well as physical barriers when it comes to discouraging your cat from hunting: a mix of enrichment activities and perhaps a double-bell collar could mean that the 'presents' stop.

Discouraging a hunter

On page 79, a study was mentioned that seemed to show that cats with a high meat diet, who were also given the chance to work off their energy through regular play with their owners, seemed less inclined to hunt outside the home, even when they were given the opportunity. This is certainly worth a try. Cats are hard-wired to hunt mostly at dawn and dusk, so you can also make a special effort to keep them in - whether with games, or by encouraging them to 'hunt' for their supper with food puzzles – at the time when they would usually head off outside. While feral cats eat what they catch, most of today's pets are hunting through instinct rather than because they're hungry, so distraction may be effective.

Physical deterrents

Opinions are split about the physical discouragements that you can use to hamper a pet cat's hunting. Some behaviourists believe that it's unkind to handicap a natural instinct; others that the rights of wild birds and small mammals trump any satisfaction a cat may take in hunting. Not many people take issue with, literally, belling the cat, although a skilled hunter will find ways to overcome the disadvantage of the bell. If you do decide to put a bell collar on your cat, add two bells, which it's harder for the cat to outwit, and make sure that the collar is the type that will automatically unfasten if it gets caught up in undergrowth, to keep your cat safe, too.

A more effective deterrent is an anti-hunting bib, which is exactly as it sounds: a soft silicone or neoprene bib-shaped structure that slots onto your cat's collar and gets in the way of a killer pounce. Not every cat will tolerate it, but if you have a hard-wired killer and you're unwilling to keep them inside, a bib is certainly worth a try.

OPPOSITE: A double-bell on their collar should help to curtail your cat's hunting habits to at least some degree.

HELPING OUT YOUR OLDER CAT

In a healthy cat, the move from middle-age to old may be barely perceptible. One day, though, you'll notice that the easy jump onto the couch takes more effort, or that your cat no longer startles at sudden noises, and you'll need to find ways to help.

WHAT'S THE PAYOFF?

Keeping watch on an older pet gives you the opportunity to fine-tune their surroundings, making things as easy as possible for them physically, while offering plenty of stimulation so they stay mentally active.

A veteran cat may sleep even more and be active for shorter periods but still remain comfortable and content.

Ageing well

Cats can live into their early twenties, but most are considered senior at around eleven years old, and really senior when they hit the fifteen-year milestone. Watch out for any difficulties an older cat may experience when they're climbing or jumping – you might have to improvise an easier route to a windowsill, higher chair or other perch. Try wooden or polystyrene blocks (yoga blocks or swim floats work well) or a ramp (pet shops have them in various sizes, or you can make your own); provided they're stable underfoot, your cat will be happy to use this sort of stepping-stone. Offer plenty of toys for mental stimulation; energetic chases may no longer be on the menu, but an old cat can still enjoy an easy-to-access box or bag, a brief catnip high, and, if their appetite is still good, a food puzzle.

Practical changes

Older cats may need more help with grooming than their younger selves; regular, gentle brushing will help lower the chances of furballs, which can become more of a problem as their digestion and reflexes slow down. Lower sides on a litter box make it easier to use if your cat is arthritic. When it comes to food, even if your cat has always eaten dried food, it may be that wet food becomes more appetizing, especially if your pet has dental problems. These aren't major changes, and they don't involve much effort on your part, but the difference they'll make to an older cat's quality of life can be considerable.

When old age catches up

Some much older cats develop a condition called feline cognitive disorder – colloquially known as cat senility – which can lead to a series of pronounced changes. The symptoms reflect the name and may include confusion; apparently forgetting long-learned behaviours, such as using a litter box; attacks of aggression during activities a cat was previously comfortable with – for example, lashing out when being groomed – and prolonged bouts of crying or wailing for no evident reason. They can sometimes, though not always, be alleviated with drugs, which can create a dramatic, though generally short-term, improvement in around a third of cases, buying you a little more time with a loved pet. If your elderly cat is showing any of these symptoms, make an appointment with the vet sooner rather than later.

LET YOUR CAT BE THEMSELVES

Writing about cats' likes and dislikes is by its very nature generic. Of course it's helpful to learn facts that you weren't previously aware of, but in the end, you are the only person who truly knows your cat; you're simply closer to them than anyone else.

Life sharing

It's not just our families and our best friends that we get to know intimately because we live alongside them; it's also our pets. You might think that you and your cat rub along contentedly enough, but what you may not have taken into consideration is the sheer amount of knowledge you have about them. You know which toy they prefer at a particular time of day (catnip mouse for the morning, fishing rod games in the afternoon), you know that they sleep on one windowsill when the sun moves round (and that they're put out if you take the rug they sleep on to be washed, even though the substitute you left looks exactly the same to you), and you know that they do a lightning dash across the room when a parcel comes through the letter box, but that it seems to be an act of excitement rather than provoked by fear. You know so much that you're not even aware of it.

This ultimately makes you the best person for your cat, whether they're shy and back-hanging or a social butterfly with a taste for meeting new people. The pay-off is the pleasure you'll get from your cat's confidence in you, whether they're appealing for yet another treat, or batting your keyboard with a paw in the certain knowledge that you won't yell at them. Enjoy the relationship: to have that link with a creature as special as a cat is a real privilege.

OPPOSITE: A dedicated owner will get used to typing around their cat, provided the cat is settled.

WHAT'S THE PAYOFF?

Make sure you're the world expert on your own cat, and ensure they have a happy life by paying attention to their unique personality. Every cat is a one-off.

INDEX

EXTRA READING

If you want to find out more about specific aspects of cat behaviour, ownership or training, there will be a book to help you. Here's a small selection of some of the best:

Cat Sense
JOHN BRADSHAW
Allen Lane, London, 2013

A classic, accessible guide to understanding why cats behave as they do, with comprehensive scientific backing for its conclusions: if you want a full explanation of how we know what we know about cats, from early experiments to current studies, this is it.

The Trainable Cat
JOHN BRADSHAW AND SARAH ELLIS
Basic Books, New York, 2016

There's an old orthodoxy that says that cats aren't really trainable; this is the book that showed that cats can be trained, kindly and persuasively, towards the behaviours you prefer (and away from some of the ones you don't). Detailed how-tos ensure you can put the theory into practice.

Why Does My Cat Do That?
CATHERINE DAVIDSON
Ivy Press, Brighton, 2014

Instant reference book in a Q&A-format, covering fifty of the most commonly asked questions about cats. Succinct answers to many of the things that every cat owner has wondered about.

Think Like a Cat
PAM JOHNSON-BENNETT
Penguin Books, London, 2011

A useful and comprehensive guide to all aspects of caring for cats, from finding a kitten to emergencies and first aid.

Cooking for Cats
DEBORA ROBERTSON
Pavilion, London, 2019

If you want to take things a bit further than homemade treats, this book offers dozens of recipes, whether you want to home-cook for your pet regularly or just for special occasions. There's also plenty of detail on what's good and what's not (and why) when it comes to what to feed your cat.

Purr
ZAZIE TODD
Greystone Books, Vancouver/Berkeley/London, 2022

An engaging look at the natural behaviour of cats, and how to manage (and satisfy) it in pet cats. It's largely written with reference to indoor cats, so is especially relevant to the increasing number of owners who, for all kinds of reasons, keep their cats mostly or altogether indoors.